BEING PAGAN

BEING PAGAN

A GUIDE TO RE-ENCHANT YOUR LIFE

RHYD WILDERMUTH

ISBN: 979-8-9852028-1-6

RITONA PRESS

an imprint of RITONA a.s.b.l

3 Rue de Wormeldange

Rodenbourg, Luxembourg

L-6995

View our catalogue and online journal at
ABEAUTIFULRESISTANCE.ORG

WITHIN

FOR NICK.

YOU KNOW WHY, MATE.

AND IN MEMORY OF JUDITH O'GRADY

WHY THIS BOOK?

I live in a valley in the southern Ardennes, 7 kilometers away from an ancient Celtic town and 5 kilometers from a former Roman settlement. All this land was once heavily forested; when the ancient Celtic Treveri tribe lived here, wolves, wild boars, bears, lynx, and aurochs roamed through massive oaks, alder, and beech.

Not very long ago—long as far as humans count time, but not so long as far a tree might reckon it—those forests near my home were worshiped as a god. Actually, a goddess. Her name is Arduinna, "she of the high places," which was also the name of the forests of which she was a goddess.

Perhaps it might seem strange to think of a goddess and a forest having the same name, a name still remembered in the name of this land, the Ardennes. This wasn't so strange to those who once lived here, though. Those people, the Treveri, from whom the nearby German city Trier takes its name, were, like all their neighbours, an animist people, people for whom the world was full of spirits, gods, and many other things we moderns now often call fairy tales or superstitions.

For the Treveri, the forests in which they lived (and where I live now) belonged to a goddess and were in a manner of speaking her home. She lived in the forest, the forest was hers, and also, she was the forest.

Of course, her home was also full of many other things, which were also hers and part of her. Most of them, however, are gone. It's been at least 150 years since a lynx has been seen in the Ardennes, though they live not far, a bit south in Leuci lands in the Vosges. The last bear was killed in that same region in the late 1700's: to find one you now need to travel far east to where the Baiuvari lived in what is now called Bavaria. Or, you can cross the mountains where dwelt the Helvetti and the Briganti to the land of the Vennotetes, where brown bears incur slowly northward through the white-capped mountains now called the Swiss Alps.

And the wolf? Well, a ten-minute walk from my home will take me to the spot where "the last wolf" was killed. A hunter's monument marks the place, proclaiming its death in 1893, but he is no longer the last wolf. A thirty minute walk from that monument takes me to the place where mangled and mauled corpses of sheep were recently found, heralded the wolf's long awaited return.

We have a tendency now in the present, in our modern, secular, capitalist world, to look on the ancient past—and the beliefs of those who peopled that past—as backwards, unenlightened, and savage. To think of a goddess having a forest—and also a forest having a goddess—seems perhaps silly, incomprehensible, a useless myth. Yet their forest, the forest of Arduinna, was once full of animals which have now also become mythic to us, almost fairytales as well.

What happened to the animals of Arduinna's forest has happened also to animals and plants across the world, whether they are in forests, in fields, or in the oceans. Last century, 500 species went extinct; just last year, another 15 disappeared forever. These extinctions, which are accelerating and occur at roughly 1000 times the "natural extinction rate," have occurred primarily through human activity. In many cases, this has been habitat loss, humans destroying or radically changing the places where those beings lived. In some cases, especially for large mammals, their disappearance is due to over-hunting. And in more and more cases, human-caused climate change has led to their irrevocable disappearance from the earth.

Now, about this goddess, Arduinna. From what we know of her, she was associated with hunting and revered on high places. The Romans, as was their imperial habit, renamed her after their own huntress god, Diana. Later, the Franks who settled these lands and mixed with the Treveri saw in Arduinna a likeness to Freyja. For all three peoples, though, the thick, nearly impenetrable forest—densely populated with animals no longer here—was sacred, as was the goddess who made the forest her home.

A certain thing happens when you believe a forest is a god or goddess, that a god or goddess lives there, and that the forest belongs to them, rather than to humans. What happens is that you see the forest as sacred, meaning something set apart from the everyday human realm, and you treat the forest as such. Just as with other sacred things, you don't use it too much, you don't destroy it, you take care of it, and you don't let others destroy it.

The rivers which vein through Arduinna's forests also had goddesses and were also themselves goddesses. The Treveri knew multiple such goddesses, and even a goddess of the crossing of rivers. Her name is Ritona, meaning "she of the fordings."

Rivers are peculiar things. They are a source of life—both of food and of course water. They are also a source of protection, acting as a natural barrier for imperial armies who require bridges to cross them. Like other sacred things, however, they have their own interests. Not long ago, all the rivers throughout this land flooded their banks during heavy rains.

Ancient animist, Pagan peoples believed that unusual weather patterns and natural disasters were a sign of anger from the gods, a way of showing their displeasure at the actions of humans. We dismiss such ideas as superstitious and unscientific, yet those rains which swelled these rivers, flooding homes, sweeping away property, and ending lives are actually, scientifically, the fault of humans.

The increased temperature of the earth on account of our industrial activity, our "modern" way of living, has caused the melting of large fields of ice in the Arctic. This melt has changed ocean currents that regulate the temperature in Europe as well as along the eastern American seaboard. This had led to what climate scientists called "the polar vortex" escaping the Arctic and freezing many American states which never see such cold temperatures. This same disruption also caused catastrophic droughts and heat waves which cooked shellfish on the beaches, and it also caused the heavy rains which flooded the rivers in Arduinna's forest.

In light of this, the ancient animist belief that natural disasters are linked to human actions suddenly sounds a lot more advanced than any other way of looking at this during that last 1000 years. Droughts, famines, floods, and plagues were all seen as signs of divine displeasure at human actions, and we are currently living in a time when such things are all occurring at increasing rates.

When people ask me what being Pagan means, I point to this. I point to the flooding, to the droughts, to the melting icecaps, to the extinctions, to the plagues. And then I point to what was once believed in these lands—and in fact every land on earth: nature is sacred, it is full of gods and goddesses, and treating it otherwise results in sorrow, pain, and misery for humans. I point also to the stability of societies which held such beliefs, and in particular their ability to live in relative balance with the rest of the natural world around them, a trait completely absent and sorely missing in our modern world.

"BEING" PAGAN

The goal of this book is to guide you, the reader, into a return to that Pagan understanding of the world.

I have chosen *Being Pagan* as the title of this book for several reasons. First, there is a subtle but vital importance in the difference between *being something* and *being **a** something*. In our modern age, we are easily caught up in the notion of "identity," of membership or association with categories and identity groups. Race, gender, nationality, and religion are all such categories of identity over which a dishearteningly large portion of humanity relentlessly fights about.

I do not present Pagan as a religion to be part of or an identity to take on, but rather an active state of being itself. Put another way, Pagan is not something you can be or become part of, but rather something you are *actively being*. The crucial point here is active relation to the world. Being Pagan is a manner of relating to ourselves and the world of which we are part, rather than a fixed set of beliefs, doctrines, practices, or identity traits.

This kind of active relation to the world does have certain characteristics, however. For instance, it is ultimately animist, recognising that humans are not the only "persons" on the earth but rather in constant relation to other persons, the vast majority of which are not human. For an animist, everything is being and nothing is inanimate. A tree is not a mere material object or source of wood: it is a being, just as we are beings. Similarly, a forest is not merely a large amount of trees all living in the same geographical area, but rather also a being in itself, composed of many beings the way that a family is composed of many humans.

Thus, Being Pagan also means being animist, but I do not title this book *Being Animist* for a very specific reason. Animist peoples are often associated in the modern mind—often because of the work of rather irresponsible authors—exclusively with indigeneity. This book is not a guide to "being indigenous," since the vast majority of its readers are likely not living in the places even their parents lived in, let alone more ancient ancestors. Also, though Pagan, animist, and indigenous beliefs and practices are often similar, they are not synonyms for each other.

I will clarify two more points in this introduction, as they are questions some readers would likely pose.

First is the matter of "neopaganism," a specifically modern attempt at reconstructing the practices and beliefs of ancient peoples. Oftentimes, this term is used interchangeably with witchcraft and Wicca and conjures in the mind old men wearing nothing but wizard hats, scantily-clad young women with fairy wings, and lots of really ridiculous beliefs which have neither connection to history nor to nature.

In academic works, neopaganism means something a bit more specific and technical, and includes revitalisations of ethnic beliefs and practices in European lands, such as Romuva in Lithuanian lands or Ásatrú in Iceland, as well as reconstructions of Heathenry and the kind of "neopaganism" mentioned above. This makes the term somewhat useless, as there is very little in common between these revitalisations and the more farcical new religions popular in the United States and the United Kingdom.

Again, this book is not about specific movements or an identification, but rather about *active relation*. Thus, it is is written as a kind of antidote to what most people consider (neo)paganism in the modern world, or perhaps a medicine that might help guide such movements back into relationship with the earth.

Secondly, some readers may have understandable concerns regarding the matter of "cultural appropriation." Just as some irresponsible authors have helped create mistaken beliefs about animism and indigenous peoples, many more irresponsible authors—and publishers—have merely repackaged and sold cultural practices and beliefs which they neither understand nor even have relationship with.

On the other hand, there is a reactive tendency to treat cultural practices and beliefs as discrete "property" with discrete "owners." This leads to an unfortunate situation where the attempts to protect cultural forms reinforce the very structures which endanger them in the first place. Furthermore, these tendencies also rely upon a historically incorrect understanding of how people intermix and co-create culture, leading to a kind of gatekeeping based on race from all directions.

Because there is a very serious problem with these understandings, and also because it is an inevitable question readers may have, I have included in an appendix to this book my essay, "A Plague of Gods: Cultural Appropriation and the Resurgent Left Sacred." While not crucial to the rest of this book, readers eager for an even deeper understanding of active relation to the world will find it helpful.

I hope this book finds you well, and I hope it helps you find what you have always known but forgot to remember.

PAGAN TIME

Most of our life, a shifting lantern of cold light hangs and slowly sweeps across the night sky. It is a light we "moderns," living in densely-packed cities illuminated by electric lights, rarely see or even think on. Yet for almost all the entire history of humanity, it was this light and its rhythms which set the course, pattern, and meaning of everyday life.

This is why the first advice I give anyone who wants to understand what being Pagan is about is to look at the moon. Perhaps it is the only advice needed, since all else springs from this. Our disconnection from nature, our alienation from the rhythms of the earth and its seasons, and most of all our collective sense of meaningless can all be seen most clearly when we contemplate the moon.

Consider—when is the last time you've really looked at the moon? I don't mean the last time you've seen it, though that is also a relevant question. When have you last given the moon your attention, seen it for the distant, incomprehensible, yet ever-present light that it is?

When have you even had the time to do so?

When has your life not been filled with other things to look at, other things that demand your attention? Evenings after work for most are filled with the tasks of cooking, then eating, then staring at back-lit screens under artificial lights until it is time to sleep. When out-of-doors at night, we are usually in automobiles, driving from one place to another, with rarely any reason and definitely no apparent need to look up.

And here we should remember that the moon isn't only visible at night, but is also visible during the day. In fact, it is there just as often as it is at night, and can be seen on many clear days even in its thinnest crescents. But how often do we really look at the sky during the day except to see whether it is about to rain? Besides, we are mostly indoors during the day, in houses or offices or shops, with rarely much more than a few windows through which to see even a portion of the sky.

THE TIME OF THE MOON

The English word *month*, as well as the equivalent in almost all modern languages, is derived from the same word as the moon. There is a simple reason for this: the very concept of month comes from the patterns of the moon.

While both the sun and the moon make predictable appearances in the sky, the moon does not look the same each time it rises and sets. Every 29 and a half days, it is full. Every 14-ish days after each full moon, the moon is invisible ("new"). And in-between those new and full moons, it waxes (grows) and wanes (diminishes) in a regular and predictable rhythm.

While it is very difficult for us to fully imagine, consider how this easily observable pattern of the moon's phases would have been for our ancestors the most obvious reference point for the passing of time. The sun rises and sets every day, but the moon cycles, shifts its face and form on each rising before returning—28 risings and settings of the sun later—to the same face.

Before there were days of the week, there was the month, the moon's cycle. This cycle closely matches two other cycles important to humans, both related to water. The first of these is the menstrual cycle of women, the average length of which is 29.3 days.[1] While in our modern age we minimize and sometimes see as regressive the importance of menstruation, humans since our very beginning have understood sex and birth as a core part of survival. Without sex, there is no birth. Without birth, there are no more humans.

When this regular, predictable pattern of bleeding does not arrive with the moon, a new human—roughly nine moons after the last bleeding—would likely be born. That is, by be-

---

1. Not 28 days, as is usually thought. See: Bull, J.R., Rowland, S.P., Scherwitzl, E.B. et al. Real-world menstrual cycle characteristics of more than 600,000 menstrual cycles. npj Digit. Med. 2, 83 (2019). https://doi.org/10.1038/s41746-019-0152-7

ing able to predict the moon, humans could also predict the arrival of new life.

A second natural pattern important to human survival could be accurately predicted by the phases of the moon: the tides. The oceans—now severely diminished and poisoned—have provided humans with one of the easiest-gotten sources of food and thus our survival. Even without tools for fishing, the tides leave scattered upon the shore veritable feasts for anyone who comes upon them. Fish and crustaceans stranded temporarily in pools of water created by the receding tide, unable to rejoin the great oceans until the tide returns, are easily gathered with bare hands and carried joyfully back to a village to be eaten.

The tides sweep in and out daily in a rhythmic pattern, twice out, twice in, pulled by the moon's gravity. The differences of these tides, however, is greatest twice each moon —on the new moon and the full moon—because of the differences in the moon's pull on the oceans during those phases. So, on a full or new moon, the tide sweeps in farther on the land and recedes farther from the shore than it does during other times.

This makes these two days per moon the most fruitful for the gathering of sustenance from the ocean. Along many shores of the world, it also makes these two days the most dangerous for humans, since the ocean rushes in with more force from low to high tide. In such places, a long stretch of beach or rocky crags can be suddenly inundated in the matter of an hour, sweeping away anyone unable to get to higher ground on such short notice.

In both cases, humans had an ally in the heavens above them, the moon, foretelling to them which days the shores would be most scattered with food and also most dangerous. All a human would need to do was to look up into the sky to the moon's face to know what the oceans were doing.

There are other more subtle patterns the moon predicts to those who know how to read it. Anyone who has ever shared their home with a cat, for instance, has seen that many animals are more active during the nights of the full moon than they are other nights. Humans, too—we sleep less during full moons and sleep longer during new moons.

Before electric lights, people who hunted needed the moon's light at night to see their prey—and also their predators—whose eyes glint in its light. Man-made sources of light, fire and all the early implements we have made to carry it, have the unfortunate downside of illuminating the bearer more than what is beyond. The closer you are to a fire, the less open the pupils of your eyes are, making it more difficult to see things just beyond the flickering circle of fire's illumination.

The moon, however, illuminates everything in a distant, cold light, making it easier to see over distances. If you spend several days camping in the wilderness, far from artificial lights, you will see how much you can truly see. When the moon is in its half-full phases, you can walk along a clear path without stumbling, and when it is full, you can see all the features of another person's face clearly and even (if your eyesight is good, but mine no longer is) read the text of a book.

KNOWING THE MOON

Rather than some mere astronomical oddity or mere back-drop in the sky, the moon for humans has always been an ancient and ever-present guide to our lives. This is not an esoteric statement, though the moon also has been associated with occult and spiritual knowledge in many cultures as well. The moon has been our light, our lamp in the darkness. It has also been our calendar, our clock, the primary way by which we measured the passing of time and the cycles of nature long before we divided our days into hours and used numbers to date our lives and activities.

Now the moon means little to us. The people of industrial cities no longer use the moon to see by, and we consult tide tables and menstrual charts to predict the patterns the moon dictates. Few of us—except in the non-industrial world —gather food along the shores when the tide rushes out, nor do we sit patiently in forests or fields waiting for the moon to illuminate silhouettes of animals that might feed us. We buy our sustenance in hyper-lit supermarkets, walk through city streets flooded with garish lights, and have become so far removed from the moon's patterns that we often see it as mere symbol, if we even see it at all.

People who know the moon know certain things about it that, to us, may seem like magical or occult knowledge, impossible to access now without special training or supernatural senses. Read most popular witchcraft books and you'll find no end of rituals to help you "draw down the moon" or use the moon in spell work. Many now recommend you download popular apps for your phone which will tell you when the next full and new moon is, apps which will "alert" you when these phases are about to occur.

If you know the moon, however, you need none of this. It's humorous—and a little tragic—to imagine a modern witch going back in time to explain the amazing technological advances industrial capitalism has given us, showing a common person 400 years ago how to know what phase the moon will be in on any given day.

One imagines that person shrugging, shaking their head, and *merely pointing up*. Such a person would not only intuitively know which phase the moon was in, but also where the moon was about to rise that night, and how soon it will do so.

It is something I know, also. I can point to precisely where in the sky the moon will appear tonight, what phase is will be in, and how close to sunset or sunrise it will appear. This is not because I have some mystical connection to the moon, nor because my spiritual senses are more attuned than anyone else's. I know all of this only because I have been giving attention to the moon.

The moon exists for me as part of my consciousness and world, because each day I make a point to look at it. I saw it rise gold and rose in the waning edge of its fullness behind the great oak outside my kitchen yesterday. I knew where to look and what phase it would be because I saw it the day before, and the day before that, and every day it was visible in almost all the previous days of this year.

By looking at the moon, the moon has become part of my life, something that exists in my world rather than something that rests outside of it. And because I have been doing this for so long now (I've made looking at the moon a regular part of my life for most of the last six years now), I've noticed other patterns and rhythms in my life that match the moon's faces.

For instance, I always feel my absolute lowest when the moon is new and just before it is new. Sometimes I am depressed during those days, the way you feel when you are in a draining bath tub and the water is just about to run completely out. Doing complicated tasks, or projects that involve a lot of effort, feels a lot like trying to run through mud.

I only recognise this pattern because I also now know how other days feel. I know what it is like to try to do something complicated after the moon has waxed to half its face, how much easier it is to apply effort to things.

I know what happens in the days just before, the "unraveling" phase as I sometimes call it, when the moon has just increased to half and my shoelaces often come undone. In that phase, I'm also most likely to misplace my keys or wallet, or to have other apparent mishaps occur. The reason for this is hardly supernatural, however: in this phase, when all the activity of my life increases and there is suddenly a lot more to do, I'm more likely to skip over certain details (tightly knotting my shoelaces, for example, or making sure I put my wallet back in my pocket after buying groceries). This happens in the same way any other excitement or sudden surge of movement sweeps us up more into our minds and less into practical things.

I know how difficult it can be for me to sleep during a full moon, or to remain focused on only one task. I now understand it's much better to be with friends those times, to talk about things with many people and enjoy their company rather than do something in isolation. Trying to do otherwise is often fruitless, since my friends will often interrupt what I'm doing anyway because they are responding to the same moment.

Noting how certain things are easier to complete as the moon wanes, I now try more often to plan my writing, gardening, social, or housework projects around those latter phases instead. It's easier to rest the closer the moon is to new, easier to clear out things, to wrap up something or to experience benefit from something I started a few weeks before. Because I know that I am often more tired and feel less initiative during the new moon, I try to avoid scheduling too much for that time and instead try to rest.

By giving attention to the moon's patterns and apparent[2] relationship to my own patterns, I find my life is much more grounded and anxiety is rarely something that can overwhelm me. This became true especially for the patterns around the new moon, because for years before (and even sometimes still) I would waste hours and days trying to do some task that I just couldn't seem to do. I kept personal journals for years, and once went through them to match the dates of my re-

2. It's always best, I find, to keep a partial sense of doubt on conclusions I've come to, which I really mean curiosity. When you are absolutely certain about a cause and effect relationship, you are no longer open to new information that will help you correct any mistaken conclusions. Knowing we might be wrong is how we learn to be right.

peated complaints about having "no energy" or being depressed with the moon phases. Sure enough, these occurred most often during the same period of waning crescent moon to new moon, followed by a sudden feeling that "everything is better again" a day after the waxing crescent.

Whether these patterns are universal or personal, I do not know. Anecdotes from my friends match my own experiences, and the traditional lore of many cultures likewise seems to confirm certain patterns, but universal claims are almost always untrue. It seems impossible—and useless—for humans to say "this is how it is for everyone," and such claims are anyway quite far from a Pagan mindset. What can be said is that the moon itself is a universal for humans, regardless of any of its effects, because it can be seen anywhere in the world, by anyone with sight.[3]

Just like the sun, it shines on everyone, and the moon pulls on us and the oceans with the same gravity regardless our size and form. And unlike the sun, which shines more warmly on half the earth than on the other half, when the moon is full it is full sometime that same night for everyone in the world, regardless if clouds obscure its face.

3. and reported on by those with sight to those who are sightless.

THE TIME OF NATURE, THE TIME OF MACHINES

Knowing this, and knowing the moon, can act as a gate into a completely different and very ancient way of seeing the world, ourselves, and our relationships to each other. There is nothing "magical" about being able to do this, yet it is also the very foundation of any magical, enchanted way of seeing the world.

The time of the moon is a natural time, by which I mean it is not a time humans have created but rather one they have noted. For most of the history of humanity, in fact all of it until the rise of mechanical time, we have scheduled the activities of our lives not around an imposed standard but by these natural rhythms.

Consider daylight. The sun rises and the world is light. Things can be seen well, and clearly, even on the darkest of stormy or wintry days. So we do most of what we need to do during the day, all those core activities by which we survive. Before agriculture, this was gathering, and hunting big game, and migration, and building shelters, making clothes from fur and leather, weaving baskets, carving tools, burying the dead, and playing. Once humans began to stay in one place, to sow seeds and tend herds of animals, farming (an impossible task at night) and feeding animals, as well as all the new tasks involved in building and maintaining villages, were added to the work of day.

Night before humans settled into farming, on the other hand, was for gathering together, cooking and eating and telling stories and making love around firelight, and staring up into the sea of endless stars and the great changing faces of the moon. Once we became also farmers and herders, night continued to mean closeness, often together in small houses around simple hearths.

Day for us now? For most, it begins waking not to the morning calls of birds and animals, nor even the rising of the light, but to an electronic alarm on a phone. Stumbling into the bathroom to shower groggily, to the kitchen to down coffee, and then to the car or the bus to rush to work.

And night? Well, when does night really start for us? When we have arrived home from work, turned on all the electric lights in our homes, and cook (if we even still do this) on electric stoves, eat, care for children? Or when we stare at screens in our hands or placed prominently where hearths might have been in another age? And then we go to sleep, not according to the night outside but to the hour of our clocks. And each night is like the next and the one before, regardless the face of the moon or the patterns of the stars.

Another crucial natural rhythm most of us have lost in our modern age is that of seasons. With few exceptions, the work we perform and the schedules of our days and nights are the same whether the land is wintering or summering.

For our collective ancestors, the ancients of all peoples, what the work of life entailed changed with the warmth of the air and the cycles of growth and decay of nature around them.

In spring, new leaves sprout from branches or stem from the earth. For the farmer, spring was for sowing seeds, tending seedlings. For the herder, spring was the time of milking, when goats, sheep, and cattle birth their young and their utters are full. For all of them and also for their ancestors which hunted and gathered, spring was the time after the long winter when the earth began again to be full of things to eat: the tips of trees and ferns, early mushrooms, onions and other alliums.

When the summering began, the work of farming and herding became more a work of maintenance rather than the harder spring work of plowing and sowing. There was more time for larger tasks such as building and repairing, with many a day too warm to do much else but play or rest or think. The longer days meant more light in the evenings, more time after all the work of life was finished to instead enjoy the company of others.

As autumn would come, the harder work of farming and herding began anew. Harvesting sown crops and gathering fruit from vines and trees, culling and butchering animals from the herds, fishing and more hunting. Yet though the work of the autumning was hard, those days were also days of extreme abundance, days of fattening upon the culmination of the work from spring and summer. What wasn't eaten was stored or preserved: meat salted, fruits, beans, and seeds dried, grains stocked up, oils pressed, barleys and wheats boiled for beer brewing, grapes juiced and left for fermentation.

And winter? Though sometimes the hardest few months, winter was just as often the easiest few months. Little work can be done in the winter, thus little work was done. There is no farming to do, nor harvesting, only hunting. The wintering time was a time of togetherness, short days and long nights spent together with family (and often with the animals in the house as well), telling stories, doing sedentary tasks such as sewing by firelight or candlelight. Fortunately, by winter the beers and wines started in late autumn were ready to ease the chill and the long darkness.

For most now, seasons are mostly abstract concepts. Especially for city-dwellers, spring might at most mean the appearances of flowers, summer might mean vacations or children home from school. Autumn now is barely noticed, a return to school or falling leaves, with winter a time of icy roads and family visits.

THE PATTERNS OF SUN, MOON, STAR, AND LIFE

For rural, indigenous, and non-industrialised people, however, seasons still matter just as they did for our ancestors. The word *season* comes to English from the Latin word *sationem*, meaning "a sowing" or "a planting," or more literally "a seeding." Seasons were the times of seeding, the moments of the year when certain plants could be best started or best harvested. As with the faces of the moon, there are times of year which are ideal for certain activities and less ideal for others, and understanding these correspondences was a crucial pursuit for wisdom.

The year, like the moon, waxes and wanes with predictable patterns, just like the pattern of increase to decrease of trees and plants. Thus, it is unsurprising that so many cultures saw these patterns linked, and chose circular symbols reflecting the shape of the moon and the sun as sacred icons of these patterns. The sunwheel or suncross, circular symbols with radiating arms in numbers often divisible by four[4] to represent the four seasons is one of the most widespread of these motifs. Versions of this symbol continue to be part of the sacred iconography of peoples on every continent.

These symbols began to arise throughout the world at the same time that humans began to build structures and monuments aligned with the sun. Throughout the world, massive stones and mounds were raised in patterns which still accurately predict the winter or summer solstices, as well as stellar and lunar events. One of the most well-known of such monuments is Stonehenge, a ring of tall stones set in alignment with both the summer solstice and (formerly) the winter solstice. Stonehenge is hardly the only such monument, though it is one of the oldest still intact. Across the Irish channel is Newgrange, a circular mound through which a lance of sunlight enters through a small box window only three mornings each year. To the southeast in Bretagne,

---

4. A notable exception to this is the Celtic Triskelion and its many variants, which has three radiating legs. Three may have symbolised birth, life, and death. But since it is a cycle returning to birth, there are technically four, with one of them repeating: birth is also rebirth.

raised 2000 years before Stonehenge, the massive Carnac stones stand in long alignments that predict not just solar events but possibly also star cycles.

Such monuments are scattered not just across Europe but upon almost every continent. In the Americas reside series of burial mounds—some shaped as serpents—which align with solar events. In Kenya on the African continent are basalt pillars (the Kalokal Pillar site) raised in patterns which appear to create a lunar calendar and possibly also predict the progression of certain constellations. Older than any of the aforementioned monuments are the standing stones of the Nabta Playa in Egypt, raised 7000 years ago to align with solstices and predict the annual flooding rains. North of these are of course the pyramids, many in alignment with each other to mark solstices and equinoxes. In China, the Taosi Observatory, part of a religious complex built over 4000 years ago, was ringed with stone towers that aligned with the sun and other celestial bodies. And the oldest known monuments in world, Göbekli Tepe in Turkey, built over 12,000 years ago, may also reflect solar, lunar, and stellar patterns.

So, for as far back into the past as we have structural evidence, humans have not only lived their lives by the movements and patterns of the sun, moon, and stars, but have also built earthly reflections of those patterns. This was the meaning and the pace of time for our Pagan, animist ancestors, not the time of ticking clocks and digital alarms but the time of the world in relation to the sky and what shone there.

FROM NATURAL TIME TO MACHINE TIME

Thus far, I have used the word "ancient" to describe this more natural conception of time rooted in the changing faces of the moon and the turning of the year, and the word "modern" to describe our current relationship.

A few problems arise in these usages, since natural time is still in use within many indigenous and non-industrialised peoples. That is, natural time hasn't actually gone away, but rather has been merely forgotten by those in the industrialised, modern world. Also, though conceptions of time tied to nature, the moon, and the stars have existed throughout our ancient past, they were the default understanding of time for the entire world up until very recently.

What caused this change was the industrialisation of certain societies, first in England, than in Europe, and ultimately throughout much of the rest of the world within the last 400 years. The birth of the factory also meant the birth of modern conceptions of time connected to machines rather than to the sun, moon, and stars.

In his study, "Time, Work-Discipline, and Industrial Capitalism,"[5] British historian E.P. Thompson traced the birth of industrial conceptions of time through the upheavals of the 16th through 19th centuries. These centuries also saw the En-

5. Thompson, E. P. (1967). TIME, WORK-DISCIPLINE, AND INDUSTRIAL CAPITALISM. Past and Present, 38(1), 56–97. free download at https://doi.org/10.1002/9781119395485.ch3

closures, the Witch-Hunts, the mass slaughters of European Imperialism, the Reformation, and the birth of new forms of state control over people—400 years of pitched battle in which leaders of the Church, powerful rulers, and early capitalists fought to repress, restrain, and exploit increasingly politically and religiously independent peoples.

Ironically, this period of history is often thought of as "The Enlightenment" and "The Age of Reason." The story told of those centuries is that Europe—and then the rest of the world—experienced a transition from a dark ages of superstition and belief in magic into an age of science, rational thought, and truth. Older ways of seeing and relating to the world in this understanding were "primitive" and ignorant, while the new ways were better and more advanced.

Industrial, "machine" time was one of the products of this transition, and it was linked to the birth of factories. In fact, many of the machines in the factories (such as mechanical looms) were designed and made by clockmakers, who had experience with the timing of gears. However, there was an essential part of industrial production that didn't work as regularly as machines: humans.

The human body is not a machine. Our heart-rates are irregular, subject to alterations in times of fear, passion, lust, happiness, sorrow, or even sudden stimuli. Neither do we naturally rise from slumber or fall into sleep at the same time each day. Nature is no strict manager of our lives. Nor do we humans labor always at regular intervals and at equal strengths. Fatigue, sorrow, distraction, illness may all slow work; impatience or eagerness may hasten it.

The logic of the factory and industrialism, however, requires standardised working hours for regular and predictable output. A factory or business cannot operate if workers come in whenever they choose; a factory owner cannot plan production or profits if he cannot be certain he will have enough workers—those unpredictable human components—at the wheels and levers of his regulated machines.

Natural time was therefore an enemy of the industrialists, and his weapon against it was a machine that is now impossible to not see: the clock. At first a curiosity for the wealthy, a tool for the astrologer and the alchemist, the modern clock became more prevalent and more available as demand for its other uses increased. Time-pieces had existed for thousands of years, water-clocks and sundials and hour-glasses, but mechanical time was unneeded except for a few specialised professions and studies.

During this transition period, bell-towers—which had for hundreds of years before rung out to townsfolk for calls to prayer or alarms of fire and invasion—became clock towers. Wealthy merchants, nobles, and industrialists saw time-discipline as crucial to their profits, so many of them funded the placement of clocks in every town, village, and city, often upon Christian churches.

That placement is important, because monotheist religion also had a role in the birth of machine time. For centuries, Christian priests, bishops, and missionaries had fought against the persistence of older Pagan beliefs and celebrations. Much of their struggle was waged against village festivals and observances which had pre-existed Christianity by hundreds and sometimes thousands of years (for instance, the lighting of hilltop fires at the end of winter or the beginning of summer) and were often dedicated to Pagan gods and goddesses. These struggles were rarely successful, so instead the Christians re-named and assimilated ancient festival days (for instance, Saturnalia, which is now the Christian Christmas). Yet still, these festivals kept many Pagan elements, as they were tied very closely to natural rhythms.

Machine-time, however, proved itself an even better way of eradicating Pagan conceptions of time. Protestants, who had especially criticized the Catholic Church for its failure to root out Pagan ideas[6], led the assault against those holding to older beliefs, with some Protestant preachers writing popular tracts equating laziness with sin and punctuality with righteousness.

Industrialists needed workers to show up on time, on regular schedules, in order to run the new mills and factories. Protestant ministers and preachers (many of them invested both in the factories and in the capitalist ethic, which is distinctly Protestant) saw the introduction of time-discipline as a way of better managing the faithful and ridding society of non-Christian activities which they alternately described as Pagan or Devilish. Thus, both became allies against the time of the moon, the sun, and the stars.

6. The writings of John Calvin and Martin Luther were particularly vicious on this point, presenting their reformation attempts as a way to free peasants from superstition. The later Puritan movement (an offshoot of Calvinist thought) actively destroyed ancient Pagan wells and neolithic standing stones, as well as stripping from churches anything they deemed "Pagan idolatry."

Thus we are in this present, a present ruled over by machine time. Our lives are increasingly disconnected to these natural rhythms, caught up instead in the gears of a mechanistic worldview in which the moon and seasons have no relevance. However, though it might seem now that this Pagan, natural way of relating to time is fully lost, it is not difficult to recover it.

RECONNECTING TO PAGAN TIME

Being Pagan, therefore, means reconnecting to these patterns and conceptions of time—not out of some sense of mystical nostalgia, nor hope for magical power, but rather as the beginning work of all else. This is hardly a difficult work, by the way: you need only do one thing.

Look at the moon.

Each day or night, look up into the sky to find the moon. No smartphone application nor chart are necessary for this; in fact, their use will actually prevent that connection from ever occurring. The goal is not to correctly guess where the moon is but to no longer need to guess or consult anything but your own sense of knowing.

To do this, look at the moon. Notice where it is, what phase it is in, where it seems to have risen, where it appears to be setting. Notice how certain phases of the moon only ever seem to appear at night, while other phases seem more likely to occur during the day.

Glance at it daily for months—literally for several moons—and you will soon find something surprising. You will always know when it will rise and when it will set, where in the sky it will do so, and during which nights no amount of looking will reveal its face. Do this long enough, and you will no longer have to think about it, just as the learner of a foreign language eventually no longer translates words in their head.

Look at the moon and you will know the moon. Perhaps you will find you also have a favourite moon. Of course I adore when it rises gold and massive just over the horizon in its fullness, but I live particularly for the thin silver crescent in its earliest waxing. When it appears I feel most hopeful, most inspired, and most thrilled to be alive.

This knowledge will change much in you. It will awaken certain understandings about your own human abilities and capacity for perception, crucial aspects of our existence as humans seen as useless and unprofitable in our modern world. We are encourage and disciplined to forget we can all intuitively know certain things, and we are instead taught to rely on external sources for what is freely available to us all.

Start with the moon, and these other rhythms will become clearer and easier to know, too. The patterns of the seasons are easier to feel only after feeling the moon's patterns. Seasons are longer and slower, longer and slower than the moon's faces yet not as long or slow as the earth's orbit around the sun. Feeling the pattern of waxing and waning moonlight makes it easier to know intuitively the seasonal patterns of waxing and initiating life (spring), abundant life (summer), fulfilled and waning life (autumn), and diminished, hidden life (winter).

And from this knowledge and these rhythms comes a deep truth about our own lives: we pass through such phases, too. I have lived 44 years on this earth. While I do not know how many more years I will continue to live, I suspect I am just at the mid-summer moment of my life, or perhaps late summer. Reckoning this, seeing my own rhythms connected to these vaster and ancient celestial and earthly patterns, places me in time. Not in the time of clocks and human calendars, not in a particular month in a particular year, but in an ever-expanding moment of all of life's existence.

BEING OF THE LAND

Being Pagan means being of the land. Literally. The root of the word Pagan is the Latin word *pagus*, which denoted a specific demarcation of rural land. If you were a person who lived in those rural areas, you were *paganus*, a rural villager, a "rustic," or in modern terms a peasant or "country bumpkin."

Another way of describing the people who were *paganus* was "uncivilized" or "primitive."[7] They were people who had not adopted the urban customs of the Roman cities, nor the official state religion, and their lives centred more upon the everyday world around them rather than the doings of Empire and the political fashions of the city. In a way, they were what we call "rednecks," or people who are "backwoods."

7. Primitive means "first" or "primary." However, because of bias against such people, primitive often has the connotation of being backwards, uneducated, violent, or stupid.

More than likely, these descriptions have elicited an emotional response or even judgment in you, as they once did for me. In modern industrial capitalist societies, we are taught to think of all those words as insults. We think of such people as being somehow lesser than others, not as intelligent, perhaps even violent or barbaric.

The Romans thought this way about them too, especially after Rome converted to Christianity. The meaning of *paganus* became even more negative at that point; *paganus* took on a secondary sense, "civilian," meaning those who were not part of the imperial military. Thus, Pagans were also seen as people who were not part of the "army of Christ," and therefore also a kind of enemy.

This notion of a division between a kind of enlightened, civilised, urban population and an unruly, uneducated, and superstitious rural population persisted past the crumbling of the Roman Empire into the so-called "dark ages." Rome was ultimately a powerful city exerting military, economic, and cultural influence over vast territory, forcing other peoples and other cities to conform to its particular desires. Rome's imperial fall did not immediately end this hegemonic[8] situation, because Christianity continued in the cities Roman wealth had helped develop.

Catholic bishops, cardinals, missionaries, and popes continued to write and preach against the Pagans, exhorting believ-

8. *Hegemony* derives from Greek and describes a political, cultural, and economic situation where one centre of power shapes the actions of all other centres of power. An example of this in our current age would be the United States, which influences the world not just through military and economic might, but also through Hollywood and other major media productions.

ers to leave behind the beliefs found in uncivilised (that is, rural) places. Another term also came into use to describe such peoples, especially by missionaries attempting to convert Frankish and Germanic peoples. That word was also directly associated with land: *heathen.*

Heathen derives from the Old Norse word *heiðinn,* meaning "dweller on the heath." Heaths (or *heiðr,* from which *heath* is derived) were open, mostly uncultivated places that were not ideal for large-scale farming, such as moors, scrubland, and sparse forests.

Towns and cities rely on farming in the surrounding countrysides to supply their food, and thus extend their political control to those areas. This means that settled, peasant farmers close to a town or city quickly conform to the cultural and religious beliefs of that urban centre. However, heaths cannot be farmed in the same way (they are better for small grazing animals like sheep and goats, or for hunting small game, and very small-scale farming). Thus, the people there—just as the extremely rural *paganus*—tended to remain independent of urban control for much longer. This meant they also more easily resisted Christianization, keeping their older beliefs for much longer than those who lived close to the cities dominated by the Church.

This kind of resistance to urban Christianity—or maybe better said the *persistence* of older, more land-based beliefs —was not unique to Europe. In the colonised lands of the African and American continents, indigenous peoples who lived farther from the centres of urban power more easily retained their ancestral beliefs, while people closer to the physical reach of the colonial cities often lost their connection quickly. Christian missionaries referred to such people with the same words they used to describe rural peoples in Europe: as Pagans and heathens, while colonial administrators, merchants, and bureaucrats adopted terms such as "savages" (from the French word *sauvage*, which only means "wild," without the English connotation of "violent") or "primitives" for such people.

THE PEOPLE OF THE LAND

Here you can probably notice a very long history of animosity towards rural people, especially in regards to their differences from the customs, beliefs, and behaviours of more urbanised peoples. Continuing into the present, many imagine the countrysides populated with violent people with poor hygiene, racist ideas, and short, brutal existences. On the other hand, some might possess an overly idealistic vision about what the rural means, and about who inhabits the rural: softly rolling hills, quiet evenings with fireflies, and a simple life of good food from the earth, close community and family, and a stillness only possible far away from the din of cities. Oftentimes, such visions are constructed from films depicting scenes of Italian, French, or Spanish countrysides.

The truth of the rural is more complex. I grew up in the foothills of Appalachia, an economically poor and industrially-ravaged area filled with mining waste, pollution from paper factories, and littered with broken cars and other machines. We ourselves were quite poor: a truck came by each month to deliver "government cheese" and generic-labeled cans of peanut butter and beans to my family, as well as to our neighbours. We had electricity and running water, but our septic tank overflowed, and our draughty house leaked out heat in the winter and leaked water in during the rains.

My family and our neighbours fit into many of the negative stereotypes of the rural. For instance, not only had neither of my parents gone to university, but their high school education wasn't quite evident in their life. Neither of them were very good at basic math, neither could spell very well, and the only books that were in the house belonged to my sisters and to me. Though we bathed regularly, my neighbours—who relied entirely on a hand-drawn well for all their water—bathed only once a week and even less frequently in the winter. My parents and our neighbours weren't particularly racist, but they also weren't particularly current on—or even aware of —any of the "politically correct" terms for minorities at that time (they, like my teachers and also my black neighbours, still used the word "coloured").

Because we were not only isolated from the ideas of the cities and academic currents, with only a three-channel television to convey any of those dominant cultural ideas to us, we certainly would have seemed "backward" to anyone living in New York City or Chicago.

On the other hand, my life was indeed full of the romantic visions we have of the rural. The land itself was beautiful, and daily life was quite simple. My father gardened and hunted when he was laid off from the paper factory in the town (some

50 kilometres or 30 miles from our ramshackle house), and summer days were spent playing in fields of flowers and by the creeks, chasing butterflies and cupping fireflies in our hands at sunset. Winters were likewise simple and idyllic, despite being a bit hard because of the difficulty keeping our house warm and our lack of resources.

We were connected to the land more so than I have been during much of my adult life. Wild turkeys, deer, and squirrels were often for dinner (squirrel isn't my favourite, I must admit), as were garden vegetables during the summer and autumn (the watermelons my grandmother grew were incredibly sweet). My recently deceased and much beloved great aunt took my sisters and me yearly to go pick blackberries, filling our stomachs the following days, weeks, and months with jams and pies the likes of which I've never tasted again.

Harvest festivals, especially, were my favourite—apple cider doughnuts, indian corns and fry breads, and all the craft tables overflowing with handiwork wrought from the gleanings of forests and fields. Though we were not ourselves farmers, much of the culture around us revolved around farming. Also, Bluegrass music (an Appalachian music genre descended from the musical forms of the Irish and Scottish settlers of those mountains) was everywhere, even though I didn't particularly care for it.

While my grandmother and her sisters were nominally Christian, they had some beliefs that were not traditionally

Christian, especially about ghosts and the healing properties of certain plants. They also had some surprisingly "liberal" beliefs about homosexuality ("sometimes God just makes men want to be with men"). They didn't know much about science and nothing about international politics, but they had a kind of earthy wisdom which was much more relevant to their lives and those around them than any academic theories were.

To anyone outside such a world, we no doubt seemed backwards and ignorant. Our view of the cities, on the other hand, was one both of complete bafflement and awe. How could people live so cramped together? When did they have time to go hike up the hills, or to idle on a rowboat along the creeks, or go swimming at the swimming hole? But also, what was it like for them to just go to the store and find anything in the world they might want? What was it like to have so many clothing stores, and fast food restaurants, and buses to take you where you wanted to go whenever you wanted?

This sort of divide is much like the divide between the ancient pagans and the dwellers of the Roman *civitas*, or the town dwellers in the Holy Roman Empire and the heathen. No doubt it was also similar to the divide between those who dwelt in the imperial cities of the Incan and Mayan empires and those who kept to the rainforests and tiny villages on the slopes of mountains. From the moment there began to be cities, there were always those who lived in them and those who didn't.

THE RHYTHMS OF THE LAND

The key point to remember in all this is that Pagan referred to people who lived more by the land and were less influenced by the current political, religious, cultural, and economic ideas of the urban centres. They were not "civilised," meaning their behaviours, actions, and beliefs did not conform with civilisational norms.

Empires rise and fall; however, this kind of rural, "uncivilised" relationship to the land—a relationship called variously Pagan, heathen, primitive, savage, and many other names in many other cultures—persists. If anything, it does not only persist, it seems to be the human default, with the sprawling urban centres of modern industrial capitalist society to be the aberration.[9]

Being Pagan, then, is being connected to the land in a way that stands outside of—and often in opposition to—the concerns of the urban and of Empire. Even though the official histories of humanity always focus on them, empires and the cities they form are mere temporary interruptions to a more organic and mostly unwritten history of human life.

It is a history of relationship to land, of connection to it, of life lived in relative harmony with the nature of which humans are but one small part. It is not just a history, however,

9. The current official estimates are that 55% of the people in the world now live in cities, the highest percentage there has ever been in human history.

but a still-living reality for much of the world, and one we can still connect to and become part of.

Reconnecting to the land first of all requires reconnecting to a Pagan sense of time, as was discussed in the previous chapter. The reason we start there is because it is the time of the land itself, the rhythms by which the land breathes, grows, dies back, and comes alive again. The seasons determine the cycles of trees, plants, and animals, just as the moon tugs on the oceans and the water within our own bodies.

This sense of time, the time of the land, is not the time of Empire nor of the political and cultural reach of the cities. Modern or "machine" time imposes its demands not just on humans but on the land itself, distorting our relationship to land and our ability to understand it.

One place we can see this quite clearly is the way we now look at food, which comes from land. We moderns have come to expect the same foods to be available all year, regardless the season. The time of land, on the other hand, tells us when a blackberry is ripest, when the animals of forest and field are giving milk or can be hunted or culled best with the least disturbance to their herds' survival. It tells us when certain birds are making their nests, when salmon swim up rivers from the sea to spawn, when the starchy and sugar-rich roots of carrot, potato, turnip, onions, garlics, and beets are best unearthed. The time of land tells us when fruits are sweetest on the branch and vine, when nuts are fullest and ready for roasting. And it tells us when all such foods will dwindle into scarcity, the first chill winds heralding winter and calling us to store what is left for long cold months of want.

This is part of the Pagan connection to land, which is also the Pagan connection to the time of the land. Food is at the most basic level of human survival—the most foundational —and the land itself sounds out the rhythm of our survival.

This is not the only rhythm from the land humans learned to hear: the sounds of wind through leaf, the calls of animals in forests, and the rush of water were all likely the guides to our first primitive words, the first noises we learned to mimic in order to convey meaning to others.[10] The means that the sounds of the land around us were the very foundation of human communication, from which all culture and society after it arose. Now, sadly, we rarely hear these noises, and instead find our ears full of the sounds of digitally-recorded voices, the engines of cars, sirens, the blare of televisions, and omnipresent recorded music.

THE CHARACTER OF THE LAND

The land did not just shape our early language, but still shapes our personalities, our ways of knowing, and our very thoughts themselves. Stand at the edge of the sea and talk to a friend. Hear how your voice changes, how what you speak of

10. There is a beautiful discussion of this as it relates to indigenous language loss in Elm, S. (2019). *The Dead Hermes Epistolary.* Gods&Radicals Press.

is unlike what you discuss in a bar or cafe. Walk through a forest for hours and note the shift of your thoughts, how certain ideas seem not only irrelevant but unthinkable in such places. Feel the sun on your skin in an open vast field and consider whether your inner landscape feels closed or suddenly vast—sometimes almost too vast. Try to think the same thoughts at the foot of a mountain as you would at its pinnacle, and notice the difference.

Land has character, or is itself a kind of character[11] reflecting in or manifesting through the people who live there. Consider the stereotypes we have of fishermen, those who live close to and by means of the sea. Gruff, grizzled, hearty, stoic, their personalities shaped by the mutability of the ocean's will and moods. Compare such a stereotype to that of hill folk, the sort of people you might encounter in Appalachia, or the mountainous regions in the American West, or the mountains in Wales, or the Basque people in Spain. Such people are often seen as very strange to outsiders, their extreme independence and self-reliance coming across as hostile to strangers. Think on such characteristics, and imagine how living amongst massive hills which constantly veil the horizon might shape your view of the land and peoples beyond them.

Compare all these with the stereotype of the imposing but good-hearted and loud Texan, or Saharan, or Arabian, and you begin to understand the character of those who live in

---

11. From an ancient and possibly pre-Greek word that denoted a kind of stamping tool used to mark things or people (as in a tattoo). The character of a land is its defining mark, the thing which distinguishes it from other lands.

wide-open and dry lands. And yet one more, the Mediterranean, and also the Caribbean (especially the Cuban and the Puerto Rican), and the coastal south-east Asian, with their raucous, fiery, and almost aggressively friendly temperaments that will turn a stoic stranger into an instant friend and perhaps also a temporary alcoholic. These are the stereotypical markings of coastal peoples in humid, sun-drenched, and hospitable climates.

A typical way of understanding such differences is to look towards ancestry or cultural norms, writing the land out as a character within the stories of peoples. Regardless, we elsewhere understand that the land shapes our experiences, and more so that the land itself has a taste. Consider the French concept of *terroir*, the cultural knowledge that certain things taste differently and better when grown in certain regions. There are cheeses that cannot be reproduced outside of the region which birthed them, because certain microbes and fungi only exist in those places. Likewise, wines taste completely different when the same grapes are grown in one region (for instance, the Champagne region) versus others. There is a massive difference in the taste of Parmesan cheese f(rom the Parma region in Italy) from any other replication produced elsewhere, because the milk from cows in Parma tastes different from the milk from cows in the rest of the world.

The secret to these differences is the land itself, specifically the soil and water. The combination of minerals are different in some places than they are elsewhere, changing subtle qualities of the grains, grasses, and the animals which feed upon them. For instance, in the region of Normandy near the fabled island abbey of Mont St. Michel, there is a kind of lamb the French call *de pré-salé*. The meat from sheep who graze upon the tideland grasses there tastes completely different from anywhere else, not because the sheep are different but because the grass they eat is salty. Coffee grown in Nicaragua or Peru each has a different taste from coffee grown in Ethiopia or Indonesia, despite the coffee itself being the same species. This is on account of differences in mineral contents of the local water and significant differences in soil composition, the land manifesting its character in the character of the plants.

While Pagan, animist, and indigenous peoples have often understood this, we moderns now think we are different from the animal and plant world, that somehow the land shapes us less than it does everything else (if we remember that the land shapes anything at all). More so, we forget even that we rely upon the land, that we are part of it, literally composed of elements we draw from the air, water, and soil around us. We take in carbon, hydrogen, and oxygen each time we eat a carbohydrate, and those same elements plus nitrogen whenever we eat a protein. Those our bodies then uses to ignite all our physical actions and construct new cells (for instance skin and hair, which is hydrogen, oxygen, carbon, nitrogen, and sulphur). On top of those are minerals and other substances, and the microbes which inhabit our intestinal tract and aid in digestion, as well as many other things we do not yet have the scientific knowledge to quantify.

The elements, the minerals, and the microbes from which we are composed come from the land and are themselves part of the land, along with all those who dwell there with us. Industrial agriculture and food production has displaced our direct relationship to that land, making food "cheaper" for us but altering our localised economies of mineral and elemental exchange. Despite this, we generally drink water from aquifers close by and breathe the air directly around us, so we still maintain some degree of direct relationship to our immediate environment.

RECONNECTING TO LAND

Reconnecting to the land requires reconnecting to this physical exchange between ourselves and the actual living world where we live. "Eating local," while a faddish and expensive trend for urban hipsters, has been the default relational state for humans since we existed. To reclaim this relationship, little money and no specialised restaurants are needed. A pot of herbs grown in local soil (even if it is potentially polluted urban dirt) is the simplest way of doing this for the city dweller who lives far from the rural. A garden if one has space is a more significant way, as is learning to forage the countless edible plants and flowers that grow in any locality.

Though the relationship of humans to land often starts with the food we eat to survive, this is but the most basic and primary of our connections. Few of us in the modern world know the shape of the land where we live, what else lives there with us, what its history has been, and how its existence influences and shapes the way we think and interact with each other.

An easy way to rediscover this is to go for a walk. Walking is not only a means to get from one place to another, but a way of experiencing the land through the human body. Walking slow, meandering, strolling, and rambling all are better ways to experience the land where you live than walking fast and with purpose. Walk slowly, and note the way your body feels when you pass certain places, let your eyes and ears rest upon certain visions and sounds you haven't noticed previously. Notice what lives in specific trees and shrubs, how they grow and in what patterns and cycles, especially over time.

Explore the land around you, and explore your inner world while you explore the outer world. Note the way certain thoughts change, certain emotions come or disappear. Cities can be very fraught and difficult places for this sort of exploration, with moments of sudden despair or extreme anxiety suddenly arising "out of nowhere" when you pass certain streets or sites.[12] Despite this, if you live in a city, this is the land which shapes you, so start here rather than traveling long distances to "experience" nature.

You notice other things when you walk through the land. Specific places seem to affect your thoughts, shaping the particular ones in your head at that moment. Some places make you feel good, or sad, or hopeful, or irritated.

12. Though these often have specific reasons, if you are new to this sort of exploration, it's best at this point just to explore the feelings such places engender.

Within a city, this can be a jarring experience when you notice it. A decade or so ago, a partner and I always seemed to have the same sort of argument at a particular point in our daily walk. Those arguments often involved feelings of abandonment and regret, strange and inapplicable sentiments for our relationship. Then one day we noticed a pattern, the place where those discussions always started. They began always when we walked by a large government-run assisted-living centre, very run down, with obviously very small apartments for the elderly who had been abandoned there by any family they might have had.

More recently, I noticed something similar happen at a particular point in my daily bike ride. Feelings of social awkwardness and immature pop songs about sex seemed to sweep over me each time I passed a particular place. That place? A middle school, full of awkward adolescents struggling with the difficulties of human puberty.

Such experiences tend to be obviously human-related, but there are many other places far from humans that tend also to shape our sentiments. For me, there have always been particular trees by which I feel immensely restful, as if they are old friends or a family home. I have also had the opposite experience, trees I just didn't feel good around. The same goes for hill sides, streams (certain parts often feeling better than other parts). There have been places I am drawn to with an almost irresistible pull, and others I find myself unconsciously always avoiding.

These are things you can only notice when you know the land the way a Pagan would know the land, when you relate to the land the way a Pagan relates to it. Daily experience with land unveils these subtle differences, as well as providing an extra way of checking any conclusions you might come to. Sometimes you're just in a bad mood because you are tired, and sometimes it is the land. You can only get closer to understanding which influence is more likely by being in that particular land over many days, months, seasons, and years, and never in just one visit.

Being Pagan is being of the land, relating to it actively and understanding how it actively relates to you. No relationship can ever be one-sided, and soon you may begin to notice how being of the land is much more like being in a dance, rather than merely living somewhere. This truth, though, is something only direct relation can teach you, rather than any book.

So, go for a walk, and remember to look for the moon as you step through the land from which you are composed and into which you will one day return.

BEING BODY

In attempting to understand the way Pagans, animists, and indigenous people understand the world, there are a lot of difficulties we encounter. In the first chapter, I wrote about relating to natural time, of time seen not as some mechanical progression of clocks and calendars but a dance of natural rhythms. In the second chapter, I discussed the Pagan relationship to land, seeing land as something which has its own sense of time and its own character which manifests through those who live in it.

For both of those concepts, I pointed to the difficulties we "moderns" encounter when trying to access this knowledge. So much of our lives now are defined by machines and the urban that we rarely even have moments to encounter the land or these other rhythms of time.

It can be hard for us to pin down precisely why these ideas are now so foreign to our lives, and even harder to notice at all that there was another way of seeing the world. This process is often called "disenchantment," the sense that the magic or meaning has gone out of the world and cannot return. That's one reason why many Pagans now focus on "re-enchantment," on becoming more aware of the magic of the world and our lives.

There is another term for all of this, one that comes not from any mystical tradition but actually from Karl Marx: *alienation*. Alienation is a word used to describe what happens when something suddenly becomes foreign or strange to you, especially when previously that thing was a part of you, or you were a part of it.

Alienation comes from a Latin word that means "other," and came to mean later the idea of "belonging to something else." Something that was *alienus* was from somewhere else or belonged to another place, whether that was a person, an idea, or an object. Thus, a traveller from outside of the Roman Empire was alien because they were from other lands, and that traveler's ideas, belongings, and ways of acting would also be considered alien because they came from elsewhere. Basically, anything alien was something that didn't belong or was not part of the society or "us."

When something is alienating *to* us, it makes us feel different, confused, disconnected. We might say we feel "alienated" from our friends or community, or that a political idea is alienating because it focuses on differences and therefore disconnects people from each other.

Alienation is a good word to describe our experiences from the land and natural rhythms of time. We are alienated from the land and these conceptions of time because they seem strange to us, as if they are foreign things. Another way of putting this, though, is that it is *we* who have become foreign to the land and natural rhythms of time, because we now are part of a worldview that doesn't believe these things matter any more.

Either way you put it, this concept of alienation accurately describes another thing we have become disconnected from, maybe the most difficult Pagan truth for us to comprehend. That truth?

We do not have bodies. We *are* bodies.

WHEN VERBS BECOME NOUNS

This can be an incredibly difficult idea to grasp, so we'll take a slight detour to talk about language instead.

Every known language in the world has two primary kinds of words, what we call "nouns" and "verbs." A noun is a name for something specific, while verbs describe some sort of action. There are a third and fourth type of word which are much rarer in many languages: adjectives (words that describe a thing) and adverbs (words that describe an action).

Languages spoken by indigenous peoples, by ancient cultures (especially animist ones), and ancient languages that were primarily oral tend to use many more verbs than most modern languages do. On the other hand, our modern languages (like English, French, Mandarin) use many more nouns than verbs.

The reason for this is that those older and indigenous cultures were primarily oral cultures, rather than literate (written) cultures. Oral cultures—even ones which also use writing—put a priority on the spoken version of the language, rather than static, written versions. Oral cultures also tend to speak more in the present tense (some such languages do not even possess a "past" or "future" tense) and convey ideas through concrete terms, rather than abstract ideas. On the other hand, literate cultures tend to speak of the world in more abstract, conceptual ways.

A strange thing happens when a culture adopts writing. The more symbolic and abstract their language becomes, the more they begin to turn verbs into nouns. This shift changes the way certain things are thought about in some surprising ways.

One of the easiest places to show this is in many older English words with Germanic roots.[13] For instance, take the words "thirst" and "hunger," both of which are intimately related to human existence and survival.

In English now, we say "I am thirsty" or "I am hungry." In these expressions, thirsty and hungry are adjectives, because they describe a noun (the "I" in the sentences), and the verb

13. English is a hybrid language, a mix of Germanic and Romance (Latin) roots, created through the Norman (French-speaking) invasion and occupation of the Anglo-Saxon speaking inhabitants of England.

("am," to be) is used to connect them. Thirst and hunger are now both nouns that describe an abstract concept or state of being. Thirsty and hungry, then, are words that describe experiencing that state.

Oddly, though, these two words were originally words that defined an action. That is, they were once verbs, something we can see in archaic and rare uses of English (for instance, from the Christian Bible, "blessed are those who hunger and thirst for righteousness"). So, hunger and thirst were not something you were or had, but something you did. You hungered and thirsted, which is to say you desired food and desired water.

Consider what this change means, and what the difference between "thirsting" and being "thirsty" really is. Thirsty is a passive state, a condition that needs to be resolved. It is something that has happened to you, rather than something you are really a part of. On the other hand, thirsting for water is an active state. It is not happening to you, it is something you do. It is part of your desiring, your active agency in the world.

HOW WE CAME TO "HAVE" BODIES

This shift in our way of thinking—from active participation in the world to things that are acted upon—is the same thing that has happened to our understanding of our bodies. Just as we externalised hunger and thirst, turning it from something we do to something we have, we have externalised our bodies and separating them from ourselves, made them something we have, rather than the terrain of all our active engagement with the world.

This shift came about through several historical changes in our cosmology, our way of seeing the world and our place within it. The first of these shifts came through prioritisation of the written word over oral tradition, starting with the Greeks. During that change, many crucial ideas became abstracted, became "static" things rather than active processes.

One such idea was that of nature itself. As the writer Kadmus notes in his book, *True To The Earth*:

> Our later concept of nature being structured through balance and law make it possible to talk about nature as a stable order. The Ancient Greek concept of nature, on the other hand, derives from the process of growing. In oral Archaic Greek (as preserved in Homer), there is no noun for "nature" but only a verbal form. The equivalent in English would be having "naturing" but no word for "nature." In Archaic Greek, the term is *phuo*, and it roughly means "to bring forth or produce." In fact, the history of the term "nature" is much the same, deriving from the Latin verb *nasci*, "to be born." For the Romans (who thought in Latin), nature is what is born and bears future generations. Similarly, in Greek, there is a general activity of bringing forth and producing, which later becomes the noun *phusis* which became translated into Latin as *natura*.[14]

14. Kadmus (2018). *True To The Earth*. Gods&Radicals Press

That is, our very way of thinking about nature itself changed from the idea that it was an active process (naturing) to a static, external object. This shift came about in both Greek and Roman cultures at the point when the written form of language became more important than the oral form.

This same change happened also in other European languages later. The Germanic languages, for instance, saw a shift between verbing the world (that is, seeing the world as full of active processes) to nouning the world (seeing the world as full of static states and concepts) after the forced conversions of Germanic peoples to Christianity.

That brings us to the second major change that shifted the way we thought about the world. Christianity, which is a monotheistic religion, prioritises written language and static concepts over a sense of active processes. In addition, the monotheistic cosmology itself is static, with a singular unchanging God who exists outside of nature because he created it.

This framework creates a duality—and an oppositional one—between the physical world and consciousness. God, as the all-knowing figure, is not part of nature nor made from nature, but is wholly external to it. Thus, thought is something external to nature, since God is the ultimate thinking being.

This means that our own thoughts, our own conscious existence, is also somehow external from the nature from which our bodies are composed. You can see this best in the Christian idea of the soul, which is different from Greek and other Pagan ideas of the soul. The soul in Christianity is something eternal that stands outside of nature. That is, humans have souls, but those souls are separate from their existence as natural beings and separate from nature itself.

In the Pagan understandings, the soul is also part of nature. For the Greeks, the soul was also a body, a body that continued in its existence even after the human body it was part of died. The difference goes a little further, though, because the Greeks didn't really see dead bodies as really dead.

Kadmus explains this point as well in his book:

> Pagan animism understands everything that exists in terms of living bodies. The more common distinctions between living and dead are actually distinctions between types of bodies and the changes that occur to bodies, such that nothing is ever "dead" in an absolute sense but only dead to a certain type of life.
>
> This conception of the body is the origin of the idea that the "sum is greater than the whole of its parts." A body is not an arrangement constituted out of parts, but rather is a whole that alone constitutes the parts of which it is made. A hand cannot be a hand without a body; it is not possible to put together a collection of various body parts pre-existing the body to create a total body.
>
> The same goes for the body that is the earth, and the many other bodies that make up the cosmos. One can't have a mountain without a valley, and without a range or plain. One can't have a river without the land through which it passes, or a tree without the earth it grips and sky it upholds. [15]

15. Again from Kadmus (2018). *True To The Earth*. Gods&Radicals Press. I highly recommend this book.

If this seems difficult to grasp, consider a famous Greek thought puzzle called the "Ship of Theseus." In that puzzle, there is a ship which, after years and years, comes to have every part of it—its oars, its sails, the wooden boards, even its crew—fully replaced. The question is: *is it still the same ship?*

We can ask this same question about ourselves as well. I am 44 years old. My body looks completely different from what it did when I was born. I do not have the same hair. The vast majority of the cells that make up my body have been replaced many times since then.[16] I have lived in many places, had many different sets of friends and relationships, have done many different kinds of work, and have fully changed many things about myself many, many times. Am I still the same person I was?

The Pagan answer to this question is a laugh, because in the Pagan cosmology, the body is a much larger and dynamic thing than in our modern understanding. Body itself is a process, not just a static object, the same way that nature is an active force, not an abstract and unchanging concept.

Besides the shift from oral to written cultures and the dominance of monotheist religion, a third major change finalized this shift from a Pagan view of body to the view of body as an external object we "have" instead of something we "are." That change was the birth of industrial capitalism and the mechanistic worldview, which is the worldview we live in now.

16. All the cells that make up the body die and are regenerated multiple times during our lifetime, with the exception of certain cells in the brain and the cells that make up the lens of our eye.

This is shown best by the writer Silvia Federici, whose work has shown how much of the embodied wisdom of humans —especially of women—was displaced and even viciously attacked (as in the European witch hunts) during the birth of capitalism.

In her essay, "In Praise of the Dancing Body," she outlines how the mechanistic worldview (seeing the world as a machine rather than as a dynamic, active process) changed the way we understood humans-as-bodies:

> Mechanization—the turning of the body, male and female, into a machine—has been one of capitalism's most relentless pursuits. Animals too are turned into machines, so that sows can double their littler, chicken can produce uninterrupted flows of eggs, while unproductive ones are grounded like stones, and calves can never stand on their feet before being brought to the slaughter house.
>
> I cannot here evoke all the ways in which the mechanization of body has occurred. Enough to say that the techniques of capture and domination have changed depending on the dominant labor regime and the machines that have been the model for the body.
>
> Thus we find that in the 16th and 17th centuries (the time of manufacture) the body was imagined and disciplined according to the model of simple machines, like the pump and the lever. This was the regime that culminated in Taylorism, time-motion study, where every motion was calculated and all our energies were channeled to the task. Resistance here was imagined in the form of inertia, with the body pictured as a dumb animal, a monster resistant to command.
>
> With the 19th century we have, instead, a conception of the body and disciplinary techniques modeled on the steam engine, its productivity calculated in terms of input and out-

put, and efficiency becoming the key word. Under this regime, the disciplining of the body was accomplished through dietary restrictions and the calculation of the calories that a working body would need. The climax, in this context, was the Nazi table, that specified what calories each type of worker needed. The enemy here was the dispersion of energy, entropy, waste, disorder. In the US, the history of this new political economy began in the 1880s, with the attack on the saloon and the remolding of the family-life with at its center the full-time housewife, conceived as an anti-entropic devise, always on call, ready to restore the meal consumed, the body sullied after the bath, the dress repaired and torn again.

In our time, models for the body are the computer and the genetic code, crafting a dematerialized, dis-aggregated body, imagined as a conglomerate of cells and genes each with her own program, indifferent to the rest and to the good of the body as a whole. Such is the theory of the 'selfish gene,' the idea, that is, that the body is made of individualistic cells and genes all pursuing their program a perfect metaphor of the neo-liberal conception of life, where market dominance turns against not only group solidarity but solidarity with own ourselves. Consistently, the body disintegrates into an assemblage of selfish genes, each striving to achieve its selfish goals, indifferent to the interest of the rest. [17]

Federici is explaining this process of "alienation." We become increasingly divorced from the bodies that we are, viewing them more and more as something outside of ourselves that needs to be disciplined, fought, struggled with, shaped, and ultimately forced to do our bidding.

17. Federici, S. (2016, August 22). In Praise Of The Dancing Body. A Beautiful Resistance. https://abeautifulresistance.org/site/2016/08/22/in-praise-of-the-dancing-body

That is because we humans ourselves are treated that way. To live in the modern world, we must force ourselves to wake up whether we have slept enough or not. We must travel often long distances five times a week to a job where we must conform ourselves to whatever tasks we are paid for, whether we would bodily like to do those things or not. We must eat not when we are hungry but when time is allotted for those meals, sleep not when we are tired but when we must in order to make sure we can do it all again the next day.

To do all of this, we rely heavily on chemicals to get ourselves through—coffee in the morning, aspirin to deal with headaches, alcohol to calm our nerves and help us relax in the evenings. We rely also on technological distractions as well, especially screens like smartphones and televisions which "take our mind off" whatever is happening around us that we don't have the emotional energy to deal with.[18]

WHAT PAIN CAN TEACH

When something goes "wrong" with the body, we often treat it either as an inconvenience or a crisis to be dealt with, rather than something we should learn from. As I write this, I am nursing a knotted muscle in my lower back. Years ago when such a thing happened, I would take a pain killer or a muscle relaxer and hope the problem went away so I could get back to work.

18. Including boredom, which is really just a state of not wanting to be in our present situation.

Now, I have learned to look not just for ways to ease the pain but reasons for the pain itself. What was I doing which caused those muscles to over-extend themselves? What was I thinking about and what was my emotional state during the time which caused me to over-extend them? And what is this pain trying to tell me?

This way of looking at the body is closer to the Pagan and animist view. In many ancient cultures, including current cultures which have preserved much of their ancient knowledge (such as China and India), the body is seen not just as a static thing to be fixed but an entire interconnected system to be healed. In traditional Chinese medicine, for instance, ailments are seen as related to emotional and psychological states, not because the emotions and our mental states affect our bodies, but because emotions and mental states are also part of the body itself.

For instance, emotions related to fear are seen as connected to the kidneys. When a person experiences a trauma that makes them fearful, or when they are afraid (including being timid, not speaking up when you want something or going along with what other people want instead of engaging in potential conflict), traditional Chinese medicine sees this as a blockage or depletion of the energy of the kidneys. External events can deplete that energy, and also depletion of that energy can cause fear reactions to external events.

Problems with the lower back in this system are related to the kidneys as well, and I know precisely the emotional state which led me to do things which caused this current back problem. I had been thinking a lot about some situations which made me afraid and fearful earlier in the week, and choosing each time to respond to those situations with avoidance, "not rocking the boat," and not speaking my mind. And then, inevitably, I woke up one morning after that with severe pain in my back, after having slept in a bodily position that reflected my emotional state.

Treating the body as something external, as something alien to us, makes such thinking sound bizarre. Since we see the body as an object rather than a process that composes us, we see pain as an isolated incident that must have one cause and one solution. This also makes us see the body as a machine to be "fixed" or "repaired."

This alienation has led to a lot of other ways of seeing the body that would have been completely unimaginable to ancient cultures, to Pagan, animist peoples, and are even still unimaginable to indigenous people who have not been fully converted to the modern way of seeing the world.

For instance, consider the way we sometimes talk about being "trapped in our body," or the way some come to speak of the body as a "meat cage" or "prison of flesh" that needs to be escaped. Or the way we can find ourselves talking about how we "hate our bodies," and then flee into fantasies of "inhabiting" different bodies.[19]

19. This is different from the desire to change the body. The body itself is a process of change, constantly becoming. Guiding that change (as, for instance, in working out to get stronger) isn't "escaping" the body. However, the fantasies of having our entire consciousness "uploaded" into computers or transferred into other bodies is escapism.

This way of thinking would be incomprehensible to Pagan, animist, indigenous, and ancient cultures because the body wasn't something that could be spoken about as a separate thing from who we are.

Granted, many times when we use such language now we are likely experiencing pain of some kind. A person who is very ill or disabled might speak of feeling "trapped" in their bodies, and it's easy to sympathise with these expressions of suffering. Yet even when we ourselves experience this kind of pain and maybe say the same things, we also intuitively understand that it is impossible.

In fact, moments of extreme pain are often moments when we are most aware of being body. It is impossible to ignore our physical existence when something hurts about that existence. Pain brings us "back" to the bodies we are and makes us profoundly aware of the terrain of our existence.[20]

Such moments can be extremely unpleasant and almost terrifying when we are not accustomed to thinking of ourselves as bodies or when we have lived a long time ignoring our bodily existence. We can find ourselves panicking and looking for escape, perhaps trying to further disconnect from the

---

20. Pain also brings us back into the "present," into a state of direct consciousness with the world around us. That is why many mystical teaching traditions (for instance, Buddhism) use pain to help students become conscious of their surroundings and the present moment, often in the form of a brief slap across the wrist with a bamboo rod. This is also the root of the phrase "pinch me, I think I'm dreaming." A pinch—painful but not harmful—brings the person to present consciousness so they can see things clearly.

body through the use of drugs or alcohol to deal with any degree of pain.[21]

"MIND OVER BODY"

There are other results of this alienation that are often subtle and difficult to unravel. For instance, because we make a distinction between ourselves and our bodies, we often tend to prioritise our thoughts and thinking over our physical reality. This can lead to one of the most common ailments we see discussed on social media posts: anxiety.

Anxiety means "troubled mind" in Latin, and usually refers to a sense of apprehension, worry, or fear that we cannot shake. In moments of anxiety, our thinking tends to circle back on itself, cycling dark and worried thoughts repeatedly through our heads despite no obvious or definable external cause.

Anxiety feels to be "in our heads," and this is certainly true. But it's easy—especially in such moments—to forget that our heads are part of the body, that mind isn't some external thing but part of the very same flesh that composes the rest of our physical existence. Oftentimes, anxiety can turn out to be related to something else occurring within the body, a "symptom" rather than a cause.

---

21. Of course, there are levels of pain for which such things are helpful. The world has always been full of plants which will ease bodily suffering, and Pagan ways of understanding the world recognize these plants as kind helpers in such moments.

I first learned this through a really helpful friend who, whenever he saw that I was anxious, would ask me how recently I'd had anything to eat or drink. I'll be honest—the first few times he asked me this, I felt quite angry at him, as if he was belittling me and not taking me seriously. Eventually, though, I'd have to admit that I hadn't eaten all day, and couldn't remember when I'd had a glass of water (though I'd had plenty of coffee, of course). After admitting that, I'd go eat something or drink some water, or do other things he would suggest like taking a deep breath, going for a short walk, or just sitting up straight.

The anxiety always went away soon after.

After finally learning to ask myself those questions whenever I felt anxious, I then learned to explore other such mental states and look for possible physical causes. Sometimes I'll have a sense of utter despair and feelings of failure and self-hatred. More often than not, a short nap will make all that go away completely. Other times, I'll have a feeling of dread or deep irritation, a sense that nothing is going right in my life and everyone around me is just out to annoy me. In my experience, that's often related to simple things like my posture or some subtle pain or irritation in my back or legs that I have been ignoring.

As someone who lived much of my life alienated from my physical existence and often hating my body, it's taken a long time just to come to this level of understanding. I wish I could say that this is all intuitive to me now, but it isn't. I have a mental "checklist" I run through whenever I am experiencing anxiety, depression, irritation, or other such conditions. I run through the checklist, ticking off each item: have I drank water? How much sleep did I get? When's the last time I ate? How is my posture? How long have I been sitting in front of a screen?

THE CONSEQUENCES OF NOT BEING BODY

There are many other consequences to our modern alienation from body besides just the personal. For instance, because we do not see ourselves as bodies, we also do not see others as bodies either. Thus, often our interactions with other humans have a disembodied quality, a sense of distancing that can lead us to treat others as ideas, as symbols, as stereotypes, or mere background to our lives.

One place this is particularly evident is in our interactions with others through technological communication, such as "social" media. We interact with our perceptions of others, perceptions assembled from their words and profile images, and easily forget that beyond all those representations is another human body. So, we can find ourselves saying or thinking things about them—or *to* them—that we would never say in person.

We do not communicate only with words and sounds, but also with body. The language of the body is something we learn as infants well before we learn the spoken language of our parents.

The writer and physician Gabor Maté, who is renowned for his work treating addiction, tells a story from his own childhood that shows this. When he was very young, too young to understand what was happening in the world, he constantly cried. This concerned his mother, who called a doctor to ask for help. The doctor replied that he would come check on the child when he could, but he was very busy because the children of all his other Jewish patients were also crying as well.

At that point, the Nazis were taking over Hungary, where he and his parents lived. Of course, Gabor could not have known this because he was still an infant. But what he and the other infants the doctor spoke of did understand was that their parents were nervous, scared, stressed, and worried. These emotions manifested through the bodies of the parents, which the children could then physically feel. And so they responded to their parents' fear and anxiety by being anxious as well.

This ability to feel the emotions of others comes through the body. The body is constantly sensing, experiencing the physical world of which it is part. This is often called an "animal" sense, and we are taught to ignore such sensations and instead prioritise our thoughts.

Yet, the brain isn't a sense organ. That is, the brain does not directly experience the world, but rather interprets all the other senses of the body (of which it is also part). On the other hand, our skin, which marks the external boundary of the physical body, is constantly in relation to the world around us. We can sense movement even without hearing merely by feeling the change of air pressure around us. We sense subtle shifts of heat and cold, feeling the warmth of sunlight or the chill of a draught. When we are close to someone we can feel the heat of their body, when we touch them we can feel all manner of things about their mood (if their muscles are tensed or relaxed) or their health (if their skin is hot and feverish, or cold and clammy, or rightly balanced).

Of the five basic senses, touch is the most active of them. Hearing, sight, smell, and taste are all receptive, but touch is a constant act of agency. We reach out to feel things, grasp them, and move throughout the world with our skin boldly facing all that is outside of us. That is why disembodied existence through technology can be so alienating, because we cannot use our primary "animal" sense to orient ourselves. Instead, we can only use sight.

Sight is a powerful sense, but it is often the most unreliable of them. For instance, fear of falling is directly related to the unreliability of sight for judging balance at heights and distance. When we experience vertigo, is it because our sight is giving us information that is less accurate than our other senses (including our internal balance system in the inner ear). We experience a disconnect between what we are seeing and what our body is feeling, and those who have not learned to rely more on those other senses in such situations will feel like they are falling.

Sight functions as a kind of shorthand for our body, something that can also lead us awry in many ways. For instance, most of the time when we look at a person, we only ever really give attention to certain parts of their faces, just as when we read we do not look at every letter of a word. We do a kind of "educated guessing," which is usually but not always accurate.

One place we can see this inaccuracy is when a friend or lover chides us for not noticing he or she had changed or cut their hair. What happens here is that we did not look at the entire person, but rather at the shorthand cues (the shape of their face), and our minds "filled in" the rest of the image incorrectly.

Reading is of course a sight-based skill, and as an editor I can vouch for how inaccurate sight can be. We do not actually read every word in a sentence, but rather make those same "educated guesses" about which words come next. Thus, misspellings are incredibly easy to miss even to a trained eye, because our mind isn't looking for them, but rather for the meaning being conveyed. This explains much of why people seem to "jump to conclusions" in disembodied communication, because reading actually requires us to do so.

On the other hand, sight does have a powerful ability which is crucial in personal communication but useless in social media. With sight, we can judge the posture and stance of a person as they speak. Even if their voice is calm and their words apparently neutral, we see subtle things about their body which tell us there is something else on their mind, or that they are lying, or that they are scared and worried. This aspect of sight as sense is missing in disembodied communication, thus leading many times to us misjudging the motives or intended meaning of someone's words.

Something else happens during our use of such technologies that is even more subtle and more disembodying. When we stare at a screen, we are not looking at anything else. One of the other useful aspects of sight, peripheral vision—the ability to sense our surroundings—isn't used at all in such communication. Oftentimes we focus only on what is on the screen and forget where we are or even that we are a body at all. We often stay in postures that are not good for the body, slump our shoulders and crane our neck in a way that reduces the amount of oxygen we take in, and even cause long-term damage to our upper spine as well as weaken certain neck muscles, causing prolonged pain.[22]

Again, this is a result not of personal defect but rather our modern society's alienation from the body, of seeing ourselves as having bodies rather than being bodies. What the body wants and needs is seen as secondary to what we want and need, which is a false dichotomy. We try to make our bodies conform to our activities as if we our not our bodies, and thus must convince ourselves that the body is external to us, something we have instead of something we are.

22. Just such a problem happened to me, which caused me to finally stop using my smartphone so much. In particular, I would get debilitating headaches and also feel an odd sense of dread and irritability, both of which were coming not from some mental disorder or actual external source but from the reduced oxygen and blood flow that being in such positions caused.

EVERYTHING IS BODY

There is one more place where this alienation from the body can been seen not just as unhealthy but deeply destructive. The body within a Pagan worldview is not only what we are, but also what all of nature is as well. Animals and plants are bodies, as are forests, rivers, oceans, air, and everything else that exists.

Consider a forest. A forest is composed of trees, and shrubs, and fungus, and many other plants. It is also home to animals, birds, and insects. All of those things together make up the body of a forest, the forest-as-body.

This is all much like the human body. We are bone, skin, organs, and blood. But we are also home to untold numbers of micro-organisms which live on our skin and in our gut. These micro-organisms help us digest food, fight off infection, and perform many other tasks the way that animals, insects, fungi, and bacteria do in a forest. Insects pollinate plants and eat the corpses of dead animals and plants. Animals dig up the earth, aerating the soil. Fungi and bacteria decompose old leaves and other bits of dead things and return the nutrients which they held back into the ground.

Seeing the forest as body rather than just a collection of separate beings leads one to understand that we cannot destroy one part of it without damaging the entire forest. Killing off one kind of insect, for example, or hunting too many of the birds or animals that live there, or felling too many trees, is much like removing an organ from a human. Though in some cases the forest may survive, in many cases the entire body has been damaged by that one act.

The same goes for the oceans, rivers, and other bodies of water. Their health and existence are reliant on many other beings, plants and fish and mammals that clean it and keep it in balance for other species. Damming a river or taking too many fish from a lake can turn the entire system into something unlivable for everything there.

It is only possible for us to do such destructive things to the natural world because we do not see it as body, but rather separate things unrelated to each other. And we can only see nature that way because we see ourselves that way as well, beings "trapped" in bodies with futuristic fantasies of one day escaping completely.

Those fantasies, always technological in nature, seem only to increase the more we destroy the nature we rely on, from which we are composed, and of which we are a part. The more the earth's climate becomes inhospitable for humans and the more we destroy of our environment, the more we hear of billionaires and techno-futurist ideologues preaching of escaping not just the bodies we are, but the body of the planet itself.

Yet the climate has changed and the environment has been destroyed through that very same logic, the alienation of ourselves from our bodies and the bodies of all that exists.

BEING BODY AGAIN

It is not only possible to be body again, but we already are body. That is, we don't need to change all of society in order to see ourselves as body, we only need to reconnect to something that is already true.

This may sound difficult, but only because you may be attempting to use your mind and the power of your thought to become body again. The answer isn't more thought nor theory, but rather something much easier.

To be the body you already are, you must begin to act as body, by which I really mean just act. Do, stretch, feel, taste, thirst, and hunger again, and do this all with the joy, curiosity, and delight of a child exploring the world.

Most religious and spiritual traditions—with the glaring exception of the three monotheisms—have some sort of physical practice which aligns the person back into the body and away from the prioritization of thought. Yoga and other similar practices are obvious examples of this, but so too are practices like meditation. The goal of meditation is not to enhance our mental powers or to put the body under the control of our thoughts, but rather to bring the mind back into the body as just one part of our whole existence.

Many martial arts similarly work to realign the mind with body, but it is not necessary to join a club and get trained in order to be body again. Other physical training practices like weight lifting or even running or jogging can do this same thing, because using the body helps us remember it is our existence.

This need not take the form of strenuous exercise at all, but such work really helps, especially if your life is generally sedentary. Engaging in exercise that raises your heart rate, makes you sweat, and pushes you a littler further than you normally go can help awaken senses in you. After exercise, skin gets more sensitive such that currents of air, or sunlight, or touch feels more profound, while, at the same time, thoughts tend to be more focused and less distracting.

Stretching can accomplish something similar. When you stretch, stagnant areas of the body reawaken, get more oxygen (one of the reasons why we often yawn while stretching), and likewise become more receptive to sensations. Stretching also will help you have a sense of the body's existence within the space around you, how much room you take up and often how much more room there is for you to be in.

Bodywork practices, such as massage, also help us be body. We often do such things only when we are stressed out or in need of healing, but getting massages or acupuncture can often prevent ailments before they start. And while professional massage can be a delightful experience but often expensive, we can all learn basic techniques of massage for use on ourselves or those close to us.

These are all incredibly useful practices, but there are many simple things we can do that require no money, no special equipment, and no training. When is the last time you walked barefoot through grass? How long has it been since you've napped in the sunshine and let the warm light bathe your skin? How about a hot bath, or a swim?

Engaging the world around you with the senses is a powerful practice that helps you be body again. Even things as simple as sticking your nose into a flower and inhaling deeply several times, or crumbling wet earth between your fingers, running through freshly fallen leaves, or eating a fragrant meal with herbs and spices you don't normally use are all ways to bring you back to yourself and the body.

There are many, many other ways. Sitting in front of a fire and feeling the heat of the flames while gently inhaling the wood smoke. Wrestling with a friend or hugging them. Getting tickled. Taking a cold shower. Rubbing your face along your pet's fur.

The idea of all these suggestions is to help you return to body, to be the body you are, to learn from your physical existence and to crave it like you would a lover. Ultimately, the body is you, the one constant thing you can always be assured of throughout your entire life. Embrace your body with joy, and you embrace yourself in joy.

OF WOLF AND OAK

Less than three kilometres from my home stands a peculiar monument. To get there, one need only walk along a path that starts where two streams meet and ascends gently through a small stand of forest. Just at the tree line, where the sloping grasslands meet a border formed of ash, birch, beech, and oak, there stands a massive rock upon which a brass plate is mounted.

The plate reads:

> *An dieser stelle wurde am 24 April 1892 durch Herren Edward Wolff aus Luxemburg der letze Wolf auf Luxemburgischen boden erlegt.*[23]

The sign also states at the bottom that it was erected by the St. Hubert Club, a hunting society named for the Catholic saint of hunting.

23. At this place, on the 24th of April 1892, Mr. Edward Wolff from Luxembourg killed the last wolf in Luxembourg.

Wolves are fascinating animals, one of the few in our modern age to still be shrouded in mythic meaning and stories. They appear in many idioms of our speech ("a wolf in sheep's clothing," "lone wolf," and "hungry like a wolf," among many others) and even as a verb ("he wolfed down that steak"), and form the core of many surviving fables (the boy who cried wolf, for instance, as well as the countless stories about werewolves in Europe). Perhaps no other animal exists so strongly in our speech and consciousness while simultaneously being pushed further and further towards the edge of extinction.

For much of human existence, we have engaged in relationships with small herds of animals, "domesticating" them (bringing them within the realm of the *domus*, that is, home), raising, caring for them, feeding them or guiding them to food, and protecting them from predators such as wolves. Sheep and goats, for example, are thought to have been domesticated some 10,500 years ago at roughly the same time as each other. Cows (originally an animal called the aurochs) were domesticated later, between 8000 and 10,000 years ago, and chickens even more recently.[24]

Domesticating animals is a slow process, and one that changes both the animal and the humans who domesticate it. Animals who become domesticated begin to rely on their humans the same way that the humans rely on them. Domesticated cows, for instance, become less aggressive than their

24. There is quite a lot of scientific debate about this, actually, since it doesn't appear chickens were domesticated for eggs until only a few thousand years ago. Before that, they had ritual significance to many peoples and were used as sacrifice and in sacred "cock-fighting" rituals.

wild counterparts, meaning they must rely on humans for safety against predators. For the human, the steady and reliable source of food (milk or meat) the cow gives shapes their activities and way of thinking about the world. They begin to settle in place, and have more time for contemplation and to build, and also begin to include the animals they raise as part of their relationship to place.

Wolves have always represented a threat to that relationship, as well as a threat to both humans and other animals. Wolves are deeply intelligent and stealthy hunters, and except in the first two months after a female has given birth, typically hunt in mated pairs or even packs.[25]

Wolves can make very short work of animals, often killing more animals than they can immediately eat. This isn't greed, but rather a kind of future planning, since wolves (like other canines, and also carrion birds) can eat rotting flesh without becoming sick. Especially during the winter—when the corpse of the animals they kill freeze—wolves have been known to return to the same animal to eat weeks later.

While fascinating to us perhaps, the hunting ability and habits of wolves have always been a source of fear and frustration for humans. A family keeping a small herd of sheep could lose them all to just one pair of wolves, a catastrophe if they were relying on those animals for wool, milk (preserved as cheese), and food to get them through a cold winter.

---

25. Groups are typically between two to six wolves, with the "dominant" two being the parents. However, in places where there is a lot of prey available, packs can sometimes be up to 30 wolves, not all related.

APEX PREDATORS AND KEYSTONE SPECIES

The wolf, then, has always been a bane to humans, at least as far as our ability to eat has been concerned. Yet at the very same time, the wolf has also been the lynchpin of natural balance in the places they roam, ensuring in a different way that humans can survive at all.

Wolves are what are called "apex predators," a crucial position in any ecosystem. An apex predator—which is classified by biologists as a "keystone species"—exerts a regulating and balancing effect on the ecosystem of which they are a part.

To be an apex predator, an animal must have no other natural predators and be at the apex of the food chain. Wolves have no natural predators, meaning that nothing kills and eats them. They, on the other hand, eat animals which eat other things: for instance, herbivores such as deer which eat grasses and leaves; or omnivores such as boar which eat plants and animals; and other carnivores, such as snakes and other predators like lynx.

Being at the apex of the food chain means that a wolf's presence determines the behaviours and survivability of all other parts of the ecosystem, including plants. For example, by eating deer and other herbivores, wolves have a positive effect on the growth and survival of forests. Herbivores will strip a forest or field bare of saplings and other fragile new plants, and eventually over-consume their own environment and die of starvation. By reducing the population of such herbivores, wolves ensure that plant life can continue to grow and expand, while also preventing starvation crises in the plant-eaters they hunt.

Wolves also have a beneficial relationship not just to forests but also to other animals, insects, birds, and plants. When a wolf kills a large animal, they rarely are able to eat all of the beast, leaving what is left for smaller beings who themselves cannot hunt such animals. In fact, a wolf-kill is a massive feast: birds, rodents, insects, and other mammals all soon arrive to dine at the table the wolf has laid out for them. Their digestion and subsequent defecation of the wolf's prey then feeds the earth below them and the plants which need those nutrients.

This relationship isn't just beneficial, but also sometimes even mutual. Ravens and their kin learn quickly that the presence of a wolf means eventual food for them, and will often fly and caw around potential prey. Wolves in turn learn to hunt where the ravens gather, using their presence as a guide to animals they might not have easily found otherwise.

So, while to humans the wolf can seem a nuisance and competitor, to the rest of nature the wolf is the key to their long-term survival, because they balance and regulate the entire system.

They even regulate themselves. Wolves have a particular ability to respond to population and food pressure by limiting their own reproduction. That is, they will have less pups and even kill off other wolves (including their own offspring, as well as members of rival packs) when the pressure they are putting on the ecosystem starts to move from beneficial to destructive.[26]

EXTINCTIONS

The wolf in many ways stands as the opposite of what modern humans do to the ecosystems we live within. As I write this, I am watching a small herd of dairy cattle graze on the meadows behind my home. Those meadows, centuries ago, were once great forests full of ancient oaks. Early Christian missionaries who traveled through this land to convert the Pagan peoples that lived here complained of the forests being so thick that they blotted out the sun, yet now there are very few dense forests left.

All but a few hundred of the oldest oaks in this land were felled to build churches and large city houses, or floated down river to be used for the building of ships for commerce and conquest. The land they cleared became grazing land for cattle, whose constant hunger prevents seedlings from the remaining trees sprouting up into forests again.

It was because of these cattle that Edward Wolff killed the last wolf of Luxembourg. That wolf, and its deceased kin, threatened the herds here, herds of cattle which mean wealth to their owners.

---

26. This sort of behavior—while unseemly to many moderns—can be seen easily in "outdoor" cats and dogs also, as well as rats and other rodents who are kept in small cages. A mother who senses she will be unable to feed her entire litter may kill some of the weakest or even an entire litter, rather than letting them all starve.

It's doubtful that Mr. Wolff, or anyone else at that time, knew the wolf he had killed was the last. In fact, the monument built to commemorate the event wasn't raised at that spot until four decades later, forty years during which no one had seen wolves nor signs of their presence again.

The same no doubt was the case in other lands where the wolves were killed off, just as it was for the last ancestor of these cattle, the aurochs. That animal, a larger and hairier version of an ox, went extinct in most of Europe during the Middle Ages but survived in the thick forests of what is now Poland until 1627, the year the last reported sighting of the animal occurred.[27]

Extinction events such as these were rare for most of human history, partially because there were never enough humans to completely exterminate all members of a species. Towards the beginning of the 1600's in Europe, however, such events occurred even more frequently. While in Britain and Ireland bears and lynx went extinct sometime in the 700's, they were both eradicated from much of Europe in the 1800's. They have begun to come back, but other animals, however, are gone for good. Several species of bison (called wisent) have gone extinct in the last century, as well as a type of elk, several species of ibex (mountain goats), hares, mice, and even a kind of European tiger (the Caspian tiger).

Over the last 100 years alone, 543 species of terrestrial vertebrates (reptiles, birds, and mammals) have gone extinct worldwide, a rate of disappearance that would have histori-

27. The King of Poland had a ceremonial drinking horn made from that auroch's horn, which is still in existence.

cally occurred over a period of 10,000 years. That is, the rate of extinction is occurring one thousand times faster for such beings now.

This increase is due primarily to human activity and expansion. As we take up more and more space each year, cutting down forests and fields, damming, diverting, and even draining rivers, and laying down concrete and asphalt across the earth for our cars and cities, there is less and less space for other beings to survive.

This is not the only cause of these deaths, either. The toxic poisons our modern industrial production releases kill off insects, fish, and birds at alarming rates, and of course in some cases we have hunted them to extinction.

INDUSTRIAL FOOD PRODUCTION

The relationship we have in the modern age to the animal world, just like our relationship to the body, to land, and to natural rhythms of time, is one of alienation. Especially for people who live in cities, these other beings which live on the earth with us are rarely seen except in digital representation.

A place this alienation occurs particularly is with the animals we eat. Those who live in cities rarely ever encounter a cow or chicken except on their dinner plates, and thus it becomes easy for us to divorce the living being from the flesh we consume. This alienation is especially made more profound through industrial food manufacture and production, where often the flesh of those beings is processed by machines into forms that would be unrecognisable to people even a hundred years ago.

The way those animals are raised would be even more unrecognisable. Especially in the United States, cow, pigs, and chickens live in settings that look much more like factories than the pastoral landscapes in which humans raised them ever since they were domesticated.

Rather than meadows where they can graze, they are often kept in small pens without much room to move. Hens often are kept in "battery" conditions, in which they are stuck in rows of cages to "discharge" (the old meaning of battery, as in an "artillery discharge") their eggs onto conveyer belts. From there, the eggs are either processed for sale or, if fertilised, incubated. Male chicks that hatch are usually crushed to death and ground up in machines, while the females are then allowed to grow larger and put into cages just as their mothers were, either to lay more eggs as if they were machines or to be killed for meat.

Such details often make those who learn of this treatment choose to avoid meat or animal foods (such as milk and eggs) altogether, an understandable decision. Others might try to buy "ethically-raised" meats instead, which in cities often cost prohibitively more than the factory-farmed versions and are not always truly different.

Where I live, most of the animal foods that are available are raised in conditions closer to pre-modern times. As I mentioned, the cows behind my house graze on open pasture, and they are milked in a small dairy nearby. The beef and pork available in the butchers here is from cows and pigs raised out of doors, living on open land. Many of the eggs I consume come from our neighbours, whose hens roam their very large backyard with impunity.[28]

From my experience being this close to what I eat, I have found that my relationship both to food and the animals I eat for food has changed. When I am in the kitchen cooking beef for dinner, my eyes are often glancing out upon animals from which beef comes. The same goes for when I drink milk or eat cheese, just as I often hear the nearby hens in the morning when I eat eggs for breakfast.

Thus, these animals are constantly in my consciousness, rather than being separated from the "products" of their existence. This fact makes me more likely to eat some things (I eat more dairy, beef, and eggs than I did when I lived in cities), but also less likely to eat other things (for instance, I eat less pork than I did before because there are few pigs nearby). It also means I do not eat processed meats, since they feel too alienating to me now (and never taste as good.)

FROM KIN, TO SERVANT, TO PRODUCT

The modern idea of an animal being a product is the core of the modern alienation of humans from the animal world, as well as our alienation from the plant world. This idea has its

28. Such a situation is not available to most people in cities, nor even all people living in rural areas.

roots in capitalism and the mechanistic worldview, but there is a core ideological problem that it addresses which we must look at if we are to understand the Pagan and animist worldview again.

That problem is that of cannibalism. Something that many anthropologists who have worked to understand animist views of the world have repeatedly noticed is that such peoples see all living non-human things as kin, as ancestors, and as inspirited beings. The deer that is hunted for food is not just an animal separate from humans, but rather a being related to them. The same is said for plants, who often are seen as "mothers" or "fathers," beings with familial and parental roles in relationship to humans.

To kill and eat such a relative, then, is to kill and eat a part of your family, something that is otherwise forbidden and considered a profound crime when done to humans. So, for animist peoples, a sacred taboo needs constantly to be violated just to survive.

For such peoples, the response to this violation is not to pretend that animals and plants were somehow less than humans or were created to serve (as with the monotheist solution, in which a singular god declares he has made all the world for the use of humans), but rather to be in constant reciprocal relationship with those beings.

Rituals of gratitude and placation were performed for the animals that were killed: sometimes as simple as a prayer of thanks, sometimes much more elaborate. These rituals also manifested and maintained a commitment of obligation to these other beings, a declaration or acknowledgment of responsibility to the plants and animals that humans relied upon.

To take the life of a deer or a tree, then, was to enter into a relationship where the human became responsible for making sure other deer and other trees thrived. It also meant a responsibility to honour the life of the being killed, by using the body of a tree or a deer in a way that did not insult the being whose life was taken.

We can see immediately how much this worldview inherently stands against the overt destruction of nature. If the life of each tree in a forest that is felled needs to be honoured—both in the act of killing and also in the uses of those trees—than cutting down an entire forest or over-hunting an animal so that it risks extinction is an impossible thing to justify.

Such a worldview also puts the rest of the living world always in the consciousness of the humans who rely upon them. Since they are family, and since they are owed obligation because their human kin have killed them, humans must ensure they are healthy, safe, and able to survive.

This kind of relationship is much closer to the wolf's relationship to the ecosystem than our current relationship. The wolf takes life, yes, but by doing so increases the life of others and even ensures the health and survival of the animal herds which it has culled.

The wolf also self-regulates, controlling its own reproductive habits when it is in danger of taking too much from the ecosystem and thus harming everything, including wolves themselves.[29]

THE GREAT OAK

In most discussions about Pagan and animist relationship to the natural world, the focus is often on plants, on their healing properties and uses. That is why I have instead started with animals and animist relationships to them as kin. Starting there instead, we can then look at the plant world not as a storehouse of healing and magical ingredients but instead as a living world to which we have the same obligation as we do to animals.

Outside my window stands an ancient oak, four times the height of the two-story house in which I am living. It has lived likely at least 400 years, possibly up to 600, and it's rare to see such an oak of its size and age where I live.

The word *Druid* is thought to come from *doire*, an old Gaelic word that meant both oak and wisdom. It isn't too difficult to understand why a group of nature priests would be associated with such a tree, since they stand as a keystone of many ecosystems the same way that a wolf does.

An ancient oak drops thousands of acorns every year, an abundant source of food for animals and birds that remains

29. Questions of population control for humans are extremely fraught. It should be noted that for wolves and other animals which self-regulate, it is the mothers who often make those decisions. Giving more control to human women over their own reproductive choices is probably the only way to ensure any decisions about population are made in freedom, rather than through authoritarian pressure (as in China).

viable throughout the winter when no other food is available. Thus, a single oak stands like a massive village bazaar, where crows, ravens, wild boars, squirrels, woodpeckers, mice, and many other beings congregate to find food. Many of those same beings make their homes in the massive branches of an oak, which are strong and whose leaves remain longer in the autumn than many other trees.

As one of the strongest and tallest trees that grow in any forest, oaks also help protect other trees from high winds and storms. The ancient European association of oaks with gods of thunder (Thor, for example) is immediately obvious when one considers that oaks are not only more likely to be hit by lightning rather than the shorter and shorter-living other species of trees, but are also more likely to survive such a strike.

Because the oak is so vital to the life of everything around it, to cut down an oak in Pagan societies was an act much more profound than to cut down other such trees. Even an oak of average age would have been known not just by a person's grandparents, but by their grandparents' grandparents. That is, an oak was a being that had spanned generations and even entire societies and civilizations, something known to your ancestors and thus a door (another root word associated with the word Druid) connecting the past and the present.

This is why oaks were often put to sacred use when they fell or were killed. A lightning-struck oak became a ritual site for Celtic and Germanic peoples, often also becoming the place where laws and tribal decisions were made and discussed.

The wood from felled oaks was used for shrines and temples, a ritual use continued by the later Catholic church in the construction of cathedrals.

With the forced conversions of people to Christian monotheism, oaks lost much of their sacred sense and became used more often for houses. This was not an immediate process, however, especially in Frankish and other Germanic lands. Missionaries were ordered to cut down the Dunor's Oaks (the sacred oak trees dedicated to Thor) in order to force the conversion of peoples, the same way the Christians destroyed indigenous shrines, temples, and sacred sites throughout Africa and the Americas.

Ancient oaks are now quite rare in Europe, not just because of their uses in houses[30] but later in their use in the construction of ships. Ireland and Scotland, two lands renowned for their long expanses of grassy hills, were once covered in such oaks which were felled to build the ships of imperial conquest. Many European countries now have a registry of their oldest oaks to protect them, since there are so few left.[31]

Treating oaks as a product rather than sacred kin has led to even more problems than just the absence of ancient trees. The demand for oak wood in Europe that could no longer be sated by local oaks led to felling of Mediterranean oaks, especially from Turkey. With those oaks came the eggs of a

30. I've been in many, many houses and apartments built over 500 years ago, and the oak beams which held them up when they were built still hold them up now.

31. When the Notre Dame Cathedral in Paris burned down, a crisis ensued because there were no known unprotected oaks of the needed size to rebuild it.

particular caterpillar, the Oak Processionary Spinner, which is now a yearly plague from which I have personally suffered.

The Oak Processionary Spinner is a moth. When they are caterpillars, they process (as in "procession") in long lines from one oak to the next, feeding off the leaves before spinning their cocoons. In their native lands, the Oak Processionary Spinner is preyed upon by a few species of birds and a beetle which lives entirely off of such caterpillars, but none of these predators can survive so far north. Thus, the caterpillars have no predator to keep them in check, and are able to quickly overtake an entire forest.

Here in the Ardennes, where the problem is the worst, during the months of June, July, and August we know to avoid the forests, a really bitter reality for someone who practices druidry. The reason is that the Oak Processionary Spinner is covered in thousands of tiny hairs which break off easily in the wind and can float long distances. These hairs contain a toxin which, when it touches the skin of a human or animal, can cause a potentially fatal allergic reaction. Worse, the hairs are easily inhaled, causing an even faster reaction that can stop a person's ability to breathe within minutes.

Last year, three Oak Processionary Spinners landed on my neck while I was hiking in the woods. Within hours, my entire body was covered in hives. My skin and body felt like it was on fire, and even with emergency medications I suffered pain for the ten days after they touched me.

Just as the absence of the wolf in many places has put entire ecosystems out of balance, our changed relationship to the oak

—no longer kin but now merely product—has created a problem for which there is no solution that will not cause more harm. Natural predators of the Oak Processionary Spinner cannot survive this far north, and no pesticides exist that will not also kill off native insects and the birds that eat them. Thus, oaks become further endangered (several nearby oaks have been killed by them) and humans suffer directly.

These are the inevitable consequences of a worldview in which plants and animals are not seen as kin but rather as external, alienated products or problems to be dealt with. The much larger consequence, of course, is global climate change, caused by our relentless thirst for energy to power our devices, fuel our machines, and produce our products. In our ravenous consumption we have destroyed the keystones of many ecosystems, chased out the apex predators and felled the sacred trees, leaving less and less space for our kin to survive.

This ultimately endangers us, too, but this seems besides the point. Often times the only way to convince modern people that something is a problem is to show that it affects them, yet this only reproduces the imbalanced relationship we have to the rest of the world. The animist, Pagan relationship saw everything as mutual relation and obligation, whereas this way of thinking about the world is inherently selfish and human-centric.

BEING KIN

I suspect the only way out of these crises we have created is to return to this Pagan sense of relationship. Many environmentalists have come to the conclusion that in fact none of the damage that is already done can be undone, and I suspect they are right. That being said, it is still possible to return to that Pagan kinship now to avoid creating even more crises, and perhaps the crises we've already caused will be necessary guides for that return.

Returning to that relationship starts with a return to relationship with Pagan time, with the land, and with the body. When we see time as natural rhythms rather than machine logic, this teaches us to look for other natural rhythms. When we understand the land as being part of us while also having its own character and spirit that manifests through us, we learn to hear what it needs and wants, not just what humans need and want. When we become bodies again, rather than people with bodies, we learn to see the rest of the living world as also body, rather than alienated ideas and symbols

One of the easiest ways after this to return to this sense of kinship with plants and animals is to begin treating them like kin. Gardening is a great way to build this kind of relationship, because in gardening you enter into a reciprocal relationship with the plants you tend. Growing simple plants like herbs and lettuces can help bring to consciousness the relationship between what the plant needs, what it gives you, and what you give it.

Besides merely tasting much better, it is much more diffi-cult to treat a plant as a "product" when you have grown it yourself rather than bought it at a store. Seeding it, watering it, fertilising it, and caring for it up to the point that it dies is being in relationship with it in a way that would be much more recognisable to our Pagan ancestors than throwing it into a shopping cart.

A particularly profound way to build the sense of reciprocity with the plants you grow is to compost. Composting turns waste (food scraps, old paper, etc) into rich soil which feeds the life of new plants in a way chemical fertilisers only mimic. While not always an option for those who live in cities or apartments, a small composting bin can create what garden-ers often call "black gold" in a short matter of months. Also, by using the leftover food scraps towards a purpose, this can change your relationship to food itself, giving you a sense of how much you consume and how much less needs to be used.

Building this kinship relationship to animals can include raising chickens or other animals, but something as simple as caring for a pet does the same thing. Pets are already seen as family members for most people, and so this is a great start-ing place to learn to extend that sense of kinship outwards to other animals, as well.

One thing that I personally found helpful while living in a city, in a home where I could not have pets, was to give atten-tion to specific animals on my walks through the city. I quickly developed a relationship to crows, one both I and my best friend became known for because we were often fol-lowed by groups of them wherever we went.

This happened because we began feeding them. He had first noticed that they had an affinity for raw peanuts still in the shell, a food they could grab with their beaks and easily fly away with, and also a food that they could get at with less competition (neither the pigeons nor gulls they competed with could easily open the shells).

As is quite renowned, crows and other corvids (magpies, ravens, rooks, and jays) are deeply intelligent and have a peculiarly keen memory for human faces. They are also able to communicate this knowledge to others, so that a human who attacks a crow will later find themselves harassed by other crows. The same occurs when a human is kind to them—they spread the word quite quickly. So, for years, I would know when my best friend was about to arrive at my house because I would hear the crows who accompanied him, just as he would hear them as I approached his home.[32]

This kinds of relationship does not require you to have a special affinity or magical trait, only a consistent act of conscious attention. As with looking at the moon, merely including the animal world as something you consider as part of your world opens up these kinds of relationships quite quickly. I have a friend for whom bees seem to be particularly fond, landing on her and never stinging her, while ignoring all the other humans around her. She has always liked bees, always tried to save them when she sees them in trouble, al-

32. There are many, many stories in newspapers about corvids "returning the favor" to people who give them food, leaving shiny objects—including found jewellery and coins—at the homes and windowsills of people who feed them.

ways avoided killing them whenever possible, and they seem to recognise her as kin just as she recognises them as kin.

While the horrible destruction of climate change resulting from how we have treated the environment is a ready source of despair, I think of her relationship to bees, my relationship to ravens and crows, and the strong relationship many people I admire have to other plants and animals and cannot be depressed for very long. It's of course urgent that we return to this Pagan way of relating to our kin, but most of all it's both utterly possible and a source of profound joy available to all.

THOSE WHO CAME BEFORE

In over twenty years of being Pagan, I've come across no matter more contentious than the matter of ancestors. There are several reasons for this. One of the thorniest of these, I think, is the way the idea of ancestry is used to limit access to ideas, knowledge, and even spiritual practice. Especially in the United States, some neopagan and heathen groups have made ancestry a qualifier for certain things: people of one ancestry are seen as having more claim to authenticity for some belief systems than people of other ancestries. Often times this use of ancestry can have racist undertones, especially when ancestry is used to prohibit people with other ancestors from joining religious groups.

A second reason why the matter of ancestors can be so divisive is related to this first one. In the Americas, in Australia, and many other recently colonised places, very few people can name many of their recent ancestors beyond a great-grandmother or great-grandfather. This is because so many of their ancestors actually did not live on that land, but were rather displaced peoples from Europe or enslaved peoples from the African continent. This leads to a sense of rootlessness and even confusion about what ancestry means, and that confusion is how some end up employing ancestry through the lens of race.

There's a third reason that complicates all these discussions, again rooted in a confused understanding of what ancestry means. That reason, though, is a lot more emotional and direct for most people: we often don't actually get along with our relatives or elders. Sometimes this is for personal reasons, especially if our parents have different political or social views from our own. Sometimes this is due to unresolved personal conflicts, like when a parent shows disapproval of their children's life choices. And generally, we often don't live in the same places as our blood relatives or parents, and thus are not part of each others' day-to-day lives.

Related to this is a recent political idea that became quite popular in the last decade, that people have a moral obligation to disassociate themselves from parents or other family members with political or social ideas that are seen as abhorrent. While it's doubtful that many people actually cut off their entire family because of these differences, there is absolutely a sense that remaining in relationship to family members with different political ideas is not something to be proud of or even admit to.

All of this makes the subject of ancestors from a Pagan and animist perspective very difficult. It's also what makes these approaches to ancestors and ancestry that much more important and transformative for modern people, because it helps put the matter of displacement, race, and personal conflict in a more grounded framework. It also helps us come to grips with the past in a way that can inform all of our decisions in the present.

THE MEANING OF ANCESTORS

The word *ancestor* comes from Latin and literally means "what (or who) was before," with the sense of "coming" before (as in, "the person who came before me.") At its very core meaning, then, is an idea of a past person who is relevant to a later person's present existence.

In most modern societies, we don't really think of ancestors being relevant to our existence except through the idea of genetic[33] or physical inheritance. That is, our great-grand mother's existence is only relevant to who we are because of

33. Though genetics is a very new science (either 150 or 100 years old, depending on where you decide it started), humans have always understood that traits in parents appear also in children, even if they didn't understand the mechanism for that transmission.

physical traits she passed down to us, or any financial legacy she might have created for her descendants.

These two ideas about ancestors also exist for many indigenous, animist, and Pagan peoples, but the way moderns tend to look at these two ideas is much more negative than they did and still do. For instance, we often think of inherited traits as a negative, as when a doctor asks if there was a "history" of heart disease or mental illness in our families. Similarly, we tend to look at physical inheritances as something of a shameful thing when others have them, marking them as "privileged" for inheriting the house their grandfather built, for example.

On the other hand, for Pagan and animist peoples—and actually for many, many people in general—ancestry is only seen as a negative thing when there was some sort of tragedy or debt that the descendants find themselves haunted by or trying to make amends for. For instance, if there was a violent and renowned criminal in the past whom people still remember, or if an ancestor caused some sort of harm to a community, then ancestry might be thought of as a thing of shame or misfortune. Otherwise, ancestry is considered a neutral or even beneficial part of who you are.

This goes equally for aristocratic societies where lineage is associated with authority as well as for tribal societies where ancestors are considered to still be "living" among the people even when long dead. In a Pagan framework, whether your ancestors bequeathed you a castle or a run-down cabin, whether they left their children large land estates or a tiny tract of land for grazing, ancestors are considered part of the physical reality of a person's life.

"THE DEMOCRACY OF THE DEAD"

There is a third dimension missing in this discussion of ancestors, however, one that indigenous and animist peoples have found more important than the question of material or trait inheritance. That dimension is of tradition, of the countless stories, ways of thinking, the wisdom, and the social education that people inherit from their ancestors.

As young children, all of our worldview, our language, our way of thinking, and even our sense of ourselves is first shaped by the adults who care for us. Our mothers, especially, because of their constant care taking of us as infants, become our first teachers about the world.

Yet, who was the first teacher of our mother? Her mother, of course, which is to say our grandmother. So, while we learned directly from our mother, we are also learning from our grandmother, because is was she who first shaped our mother's understanding of the world and even shaped our mother's idea of what mothering is. Our grandmother, by mothering our mother, taught her how to mother us. And she, in turn, was taught by her mother, our great grandmother.

In this simple chain of mothering is the key to the Pagan and animist understanding of what ancestors are and what tradition means. Though we might never have met our great-great grandparents, because they shaped the worldview of our grandparents who in turned shaped the worldview of our parents, we are also being parented by them, not just by our mother and father.

This kind of transmission of worldview itself is what we call tradition, and it cannot be accounted for by genetic or physical inheritance. It isn't something we are born with, but something passed along to us, a body of knowledge and wisdom comprised of many generations of people we never could have met.

Tradition, like ancestry, is also a thorny subject, especially since many people have politicized the idea. Political conservatives tend to be considered "traditionalists," with the sense of preserving tradition against sudden social change. Political liberals, on the other hand, tend to be anti-traditionalists, seeing social change as an inherently good thing and tradition as a kind of intellectual backwardness.

With many such things, it's best to strip away the political connotations of the term and look at the more radical[34] core of the idea. Tradition's root in Latin means to "give across," referring to something passed along. That is, tradition refers to the transmission of ideas, beliefs, worldviews, rituals, habits, and social frameworks across generations, from ancestors to descendants.

34. Radical comes from a Latin word meaning "root."

Stripping away the politicisation of the idea of tradition, we can see that tradition doesn't really mean "how it has always been done," nor "how is should be done," but rather "what was taught to me from those before." There is no sense in the original meaning that tradition is against change, but rather that it is merely a simple fact of how we learned certain things.

Tradition, then, is a kind of knowledge and way of knowing, just as science is a kind of knowledge and way of knowing. And just as science can accurately answer some questions (for instance, how far away is the Sun from the Earth?) but cannot answer other things (how do I know I'm in love?), tradition is useful for many things in life but not so useful for others.

Tradition is how I learned not to put my hand on a hot stove, how not to get hit by automobiles when crossing a street, and how to cook a basic meal. It is also how I learned a basic moral framework, that telling the truth is usually easier than lying, that being kind to others causes a lot less conflict than being cruel, that acknowledging generosity in others and also being generous means life is a lot easier and more abundant for everyone.

Of course, there are many things I learned through tradition that I later questioned or rejected, such as certain beliefs about the way the world works that I decided were neither true nor useful. Tradition isn't authority, but rather a body of wisdom and ideas that those who inherit also create and pass along. It's a co-creative process.

The writer G.K. Chesterton, while himself a traditional Catholic, expressed this co-creative meaning of tradition in a remarkably Pagan way:[35]

> Tradition means giving votes to the most obscure of all classes, our ancestors. It is the democracy of the dead. Tradition refuses to submit to the small and arrogant oligarchy of those who merely happen to be walking about. All democrats object to men being disqualified by the accident of birth; tradition objects to their being disqualified by the accident of death.[36]

ANCESTRAL TRADITIONS

In many neopagan groups, as well as in indigenous and post-colonial studies, there is often a focus on "ancestral tradition." While they often mean different things by the term, the sense is often one of a kind of mystification. That is, ancestral tradition is treated as something both rare and located only within indigenous cultures or ancient societies. This unfortunately leads us to miss the really-existing ancestral traditions that have already shaped our existence.

Both my aunt and one of my own sisters have a really profound affinity for animals. Both have homes filled with them: my aunt for decades worked as a world-renowned trainer for guide dogs for blind people, and my sister for years volunteered to foster rescue dogs and cats for a no-kill animal

35. As with much of his writing, actually.

36. Chesterton, G. K. (1908). *Orthodoxy*. John Lane Company.

shelter. My grandfather himself had this sort of affinity, spending a lot of time feeding deer, raccoons, and birds who would wander into his back yard from a nearby forest.

Caretaking animals is a kind of ancestral tradition passed down through my grandfather, which came to him from his ancestors. They themselves were poor farmers, displaced peoples from the Breton coasts and Germanic lands, and they passed along another ancestral tradition, as well: thrift.

My grandfather walked to school on cold mornings with a hot baked potato in each pocket. His mother put them there to keep his hands warm for the walk, and then to be eaten as lunch at school. That same kind of simplicity defined the rest of his life: he rarely spent money, always had his clothes repaired rather than replaced, and never invested in anything that entailed any kind of risk. This he learned from his parents and their parents, and passed along to his children and grandchildren.

These are both ancestral traditions in the same way that indigenous peoples have ancestral traditions. A way of seeing the world (take care of animals, use what is already available rather than spending money for something else) was passed on over generations and inherited by those of us who continue on after their deaths. In my own life, these two ancestral traditions have translated both into druidry and a kind of political leftism for me, which I see as my own manifestation of what my ancestors believed.

Where I live now in the Ardennes, ancestral traditions are a lot easier to see. This is mostly because many of the people who live here dwell in the same villages (and often in the very same houses) that their ancestors lived in. I live with my partner in the house where he was born, and his mother also lives here in a separate section of the house. She was also born here, as was her own mother, grandmother, and great-grandmother.

As with many small European villages, the children often held the same jobs or performed the same kind of work as their ancestors. My mother-in-law spent most of her life as a washing woman, as had her mother, grandmother, and great grandmother. In fact, the house itself was built from even older ruins of a washing house for the large landowner who owned most of this village and surrounding lands back into the Middle Ages. The descendants of the servants who performed the washing then were given the land when the land owner fell into poverty hundreds of years ago.

That is, there is a continuous matrilineal line of washing women who have lived in this spot for hundreds and hundreds of years all leading up to my mother-in-law. What they taught her, besides just how to make clothing look perfectly new no matter what the wearer did to it, was also how to be deeply resilient and deeply connected to others in poor circumstances in a way I have never seen before. While every family in this village has had some sort of feud with another family, my mother-in-law is renowned as the one woman who is always welcome at any door because of her refusal to let strife get in the way of the importance of the community life of the village.

Such ancestral traditions might be also called "family" traditions, but in the Pagan understanding of ancestry, family is a much larger concept than just direct family members. Especially when people have lived for hundreds—even thousands—of years in the same general area, family relations are often spread through many, many villages. Those connections may be distant "genetically," but they are not seen as distant to the people who are part of them.

So to speak about ancestry and ancestral traditions, we must first understand that the way these concepts are lived and experienced are much more real and present than the way scholars, academics, activists, and others speak about them. What is inherited from those who came before isn't some abstract idea or material benefit, but rather a tapestry woven from still-living threads of memory, story, and ways of being in the world that cannot be contained in scientific or political categories.

A Collective Ancestral Wound

It's at this point we can look at the matter of ancestry and the concept of "race," an idea that is currently tearing apart much of the world and has come to replace these older ideas of ancestry.

Race doesn't exist. Race is a scientific and legal fiction that was born in the 1600's, created out of the need of colonial administrators to find a way to define displaced and enslaved peoples so they could be categorized and divided.

Before the early 1600's, there were no black people, nor were there white people. Before there were black people, there were people ripped from their ancestral villages on the African continent and hauled across the ocean in the hulls of ships to do forced labor. Before there were white people, there were people pushed out of their ancestral villages through new "Enclosure" laws on the European continent and the British Isles, who often sold the very little they had (and even themselves, in the case of indentured servitude contracts) in order to survive.

The people who came from those villages on the African continent each had their own ancestral traditions, and their own ideas of themselves completely different from those had enslaved them. So, too, for the displaced poor from the European continent, each of whom had previously been connected to place and a sense of time through the tapestry of their own ancestral traditions.

It was the same, also, for those who were already living in the lands being colonized, to which those people were brought as prisoners or refugees. The Americas were populated by countless people groups, each with their own names for themselves, their own ways of seeing the world, their own ancestral stories, and their own ancestral traditions. Many of those people were destroyed or displaced, the tapestries of their own lives torn apart by the thirst of Empire.

This is why the idea of ancestry and tradition is so fraught now, as if each time those words are brought up an old wound is re-opened that we do not remember first experiencing. For many, sometime during the last few hundred years our ancestors were displaced from the lands they knew onto lands they did not know.

Even for those who were not displaced, all the traditional knowledge their parents, grandparents, and great-grandparents had passed along to them no longer could make sense of the world around them. The old ways of doing work had changed—you couldn't live off the land your ancestors had lived in. Suddenly you had to work in factories, and there were no factories before, so there was no ancestral tradition to describe what was happening.

In the absence of ancestral tradition, new concepts such as race were easier to force upon people then and also now. Race has come to replace ancestry as an identification, so much so that it is very difficult to even comprehend that no one before the 1600's ever saw themselves or others as part of a race.[37]

Though ancestral traditions were wounded and often severed by capitalism, slavery, and imperialist policies, a second wounding was done to those of us who live down the line from this trauma. That wounding is in our confusion about

37. This is the easiest response to people who try to limit ancient belief and cultural forms to specific racial identities. Those racial identities didn't exist at the time those practices and beliefs arose, thus they cannot be said to have been "for whites only" or "only for black people." For a much longer discussion of this as it relates to cultural appropriation, see my essay, "A Plague of Gods: Cultural Appropriation and the Resurgent Left Sacred," at the end of this book.

what ancestry and tradition even mean, and more so our tendency to see such concepts as "backwards" and politically reactionary.

Especially when we mystify the idea of ancestry and tradition and see it as something that is either permanently lost or something that only a few isolated cultures still possess, we continue this wounding. Ancestry and tradition are how we connect to the past, and without that connection we cannot understand the present or even really fully understand ourselves.

THE DEAD ARE ALWAYS WITH US

On a shrine in a room in the house where I live sits a small bowl of water. It's a handmade ceramic bowl, crafted by one of my sisters. It is always full of water, refilled twice a week. Every morning upon waking, and every night just before sleeping, I say some words while looking at the bowl, a prayer of thanks to specific people who are no longer living.

While so far I have written about the cultural and social aspects of ancestry and tradition, I've not yet spoken of the spiritual aspects. Though this is not quite true: we must remember that Pagan and animist people made no distinction between culture, the social, and the spiritual, any more than they made distinctions between themselves and their bodies.

Let's return to a quote from Kadmus in his book *True to the Earth*, which we first looked at when speaking of bodies:

> Pagan animism understands everything that exists in terms of living bodies. The more common distinctions between living and dead are actually distinctions between types of bodies and the changes that occur to bodies, such that nothing is ever "dead" in an absolute sense but only dead to a certain type of life.[38]

The state of ancestors in a Pagan, animist sense isn't merely a state of having gone before, but also still being around. However, that "still being around" isn't quite the modern fantasies about ghosts and hauntings, but neither is it just a poetic metaphor.

My grandfather is still around, though he died. I speak to him every morning and every evening, and sometimes he speaks to me in dreams both sleeping and sometimes waking. A few months ago, there was a fire in my home as I and my partner slept. Neither of us woke as black smoke filled every room, nor did the fire alarms sound to alert us. Sometime in the night, I spoke to my grandfather. It was definitely a dream, but also not exactly a dream but rather something else entirely.[39]

---

38. Kadmus. (2018). *True To The Earth*. Gods&Radicals Press

39. As Kadmus also notes in *True To the Earth*: "This idea of sleep touching death is also well attested to in the ancient world....It was (and still is in many cultures) a common truth that the dead speak to us in our sleep. More potently, there is a longstanding tradition in both Greek and Roman culture that dreams come through two gates, a gate of truth and one of falsehood, and both gates are found in the Underworld land of the dead. In fact, sleep and dream are often identified with the gates to the Underworld."

"You're dying," he said to me.

"No, not tonight," I answered.

And then my grandfather looked at me, shrugged, and said "okay."

The next morning when my partner and I woke up, groggy and extremely confused from the smoke inhalation, we found that the fire had both started spontaneously but also put itself out "spontaneously." Did my grandfather put it out? I don't know, nor is that exactly the correct question. What mattered was that he was there, had informed me of what was happening, and that I hadn't died.

Such encounters with ancestors are not only well-attested to in indigenous cultures, but also in many modern accounts. Everyone I know has at some point mentioned the sense of encountering a dead relative, or having the sense that they were visited by them, or dreamed of talking to them. In my experience, it seems to be quite common for children to report such encounters, and while some adults might dismiss these stories as childish make-believe, I suspect they'd also admit having had similar experiences when children, too.

The ancestors I speak to every morning and every night, for whom I fill a bowl of water on a shrine, are not all ancestors "of blood." One of them is a friend and fellow druid and writer, now no longer living but still, I'm sure, quite around.

She, Judith O'Grady, left us all an essay on this very subject, entitled "I'll Be An Ancestor One Day."[40] Her own granddaughter had reported seeing a woman in her room at night many times, who Judith recognised by her description as her own grandmother. Then, after another death in the family, Judith recounts the conversation she had with her granddaughter about death:

> "I will die one day," I said, "and I don't know about the hugs, but I'm sure I will often come and visit you. Do you know why I am so sure?...my Grannie comes and visits you already..."

Reading back on that essay, I smile, just as I feel somewhere a smile from her as I write about her. I also smile when I think how this kind of relation to the dead is hardly new, but is instead part of the traditions of many, many peoples. Ancestor altars and shrines can be seen in Hindu, Shinto, Buddhist, and even Catholic[41] homes. Even in the secular societies, national days of remembrance for fallen soldiers or leaders (for example, Martin Luther King, Jr. Day in the United States) are distant continuations of ancestral rites.[42]

40. O'Grady, J. (2015, November 4). I'll Be an Ancestor One Day. A Site of Beautiful Resistance. https://godsandradicals.org/2015/11/04/ill-be-an-ancestor-one-day/

41. In many Catholic churches, masses are performed in memory of the dead. The official purpose of these masses is to speed the dead soul's journey to heaven from purgatory, which actually mirrors many indigenous ancestral practices of speeding the dead's transition from their previous life to their next life.

42. Even the American term "Founding Fathers" is a kind of state-sanctioned ancestral veneration.

Ancestral veneration is perhaps the easiest of the animist traditions to return to for a modern, because it requires very little. You don't even need to know the names of your ancestors or necessarily speak to them. One of the most common practices that can be found throughout the world is occasionally leaving something out for them, be that a small bowl of water, a small candle, or even a portion of a meal.

Many people already actually have shrines to their ancestors in their homes without realizing it. Often, there is a place in a home where photos or keepsakes of dead relatives are displayed, a place on a wall, above a fireplace mantle, or a shelf. These are all types of ancestor shrines, and you maybe already have one as well.

If not, or if you would like to create one with intention, the easiest way to do this is to set up a small dedicated place for them. In a later chapter I will discuss more about creating shrines, but for now just pick a spot that feels right and that will not be used for other things.

Then, put photographs, or memorabilia, or anything that might remind you of your favourite relatives who have passed. Or, you can do as I do, put a small bowl of water in the spot and remember to change the water and refill it regularly. A small candle you light on a particular day (the first of November is a traditional day in many northern countries, or you can pick an anniversary or birthday) is also just as appropriate as all the rest.

No prayers need to be said or statements made. Perhaps you might find yourself sometimes wanting to say something to a grandmother or a friend whose death separated you from them. Perhaps by speaking to them there you will find solace or comfort.

Perhaps you will also find you feel they maybe also speak back.

GODS AND SPIRITS

The most widespread of beliefs among Pagan, animist, and indigenous people is that of a world full of spirits and gods. For moderns, however, our ideas about what a spirit or a god is are often hopelessly filtered by fantasy, secular "reason," and a deep misunderstanding about the past. At best, most of us imagine that the world was once full of such beings but is no more. Or, the Jungian "archetype" model leads us to believe that such things were really just mental constructs which gave earlier people meanings.

So, what exactly is a god? What is a spirit? To answer this question, let's look at a kind of being typically seen as a pure construction of fantasy: dragons.

A SCOURGE OF DRAGONS

Yearly in the city of the people of the middle mothers, an effigy of a dragon is paraded throughout the city, as it has been almost continuously for at least one thousand years and likely much longer. The name of that dragon is Graoully, and images of it can be found carved into ancient buildings, woven into tapestries, and depicted in statues throughout the 3000 year-old city.

While all this might sound like the beginning of a fantasy novel, it isn't fantasy at all. The city of the people of the middle mothers (the Celtic tribe named in Latin the Mediomatrici) is only 100 kilometres from where I live, located just between the great forests where the god Vosges and the goddess Arduinna were worshipped. That city is now called Metz, in modern-day France, and Graoully is still marched through its streets in the form of a dragon.

Much further south from the city of Metz are other dragons. Two of these are in the lands once held by the people of the giants (the Cavarii), who were part of the larger territory of the exiled peoples (the Allobroges). One of these dragons, Coulobre, no longer has processions or rituals devoted to her. She, a dragon from the cliffs, once was venerated at a gate to the underworld now called the Fountain of Vaucluse, the fifth largest spring in the world.

To the west is another dragon who, unlike Coulobre but like Graoully, is still paraded through the streets of a town. This dragon is La Tarasque, a dragon with a head like a lion and a body like that of a tortoise.

All three of these dragons share a similar history and a similar fate. Each was venerated by the Celtic peoples who inhabited Gaul before and during the time the Roman Empire swept through. Each is associated with sacred rivers and inhabited both the waters and the earth around them. And each, in turn, were also said to have been "conquered" by Christian saints.

The story of the Tarasque is perhaps the most famous of these three. St. Martha, the sister of Mary Magdalene, is said to have encountered the Tarasque in a forest while it ate a man. Sprinkling holy water on it and wrapping the rope of her tunic around its neck, she led it into a village where the inhabitants then pelted it with stones until it died.

Coulubre, at the Fountain of Vaucluse, met a similar fate at the hands of a saint. Veranus, bishop of Vaucluse, is said to have chased her from her home and the place of her veneration into the Alps, where she supposedly died of her own accord.

The story of the fate of Graoully is a bit more elaborate. The tale goes that Clement, a missionary sent to convert the inhabitants of one of the richest and most powerful cities in Gaul, arrived in the city and found it swarming with serpents led by the dragon. He promised the people a miracle: he would rid the city of the beasts if they would first convert to the "true faith." The people supposedly agreed, and so he made the sign of the cross at the serpents, which made them immediately submit to him. Then, he forced Graoully to return to one of the rivers which flow through the city, to go to a place where no humans nor beasts lived.

All three Christian tales, as with countless others involving dragons and other beings, were part of a Catholic tradition to explain and prove the death of older beliefs, spirits, and gods. In each story, the new religious order displaced or conquered the older order by magical or miraculous means, and the people who performed those acts were then considered saints (holy people) of the new order.

DRAGONS OF THE LAND, DRAGONS OF THE WATER

Such stories are particularly widespread in western European lands, especially in what is now France, Germany, and Spain. They also appear often in the British Isles, such as the idea that Patrick (and also Columba) banished snakes from Ireland[43], and most famously in the story of "St. George and the Dragon," which is clearly a parallel of the mainland European stories of dragons conquered by saints.

Dragons are such a common theme in these stories that it's worth looking into them more deeply. While some suggest

43. Many geologists and natural historians point out that there were likely never any snakes in Ireland. We can see the resonance of this story in Clement of Metz, who lived likely 400 years before Patrick. Some have suggested that "snake" was a metaphor for the druids, and though this isn't certain, regardless the tale is of the same genre as the other stories of the old order being displaced by a saint.

that the myth of dragon slaying comes from Christianity itself, there are actually no stories or myths about dragons in the Bible except for one from the apocryphal additions to the Book of Daniel. That section, however, was never referenced by Jewish rabbis in any of their writings, and the earliest known Jewish reference to that section is from the 17th century. Thus, it is most likely a later addition, possibly written by a scribe at the same time that dragon stories were written in Europe.

On the other hand, we do have surviving Celtic stories regarding dragons (and many other stories about gods as well), thanks to the bardic tradition which survived through merger with the Christian monasteries. In the texts they compiled, we find a story about a red and a white dragon dwelling in an underground lake who struggle with each other. Those dragons constantly make the land above them tremble, preventing the king Vortigern from building a fortress above it.

We learn in this tale that each of these two dragons is associated with a land: the red dragon is the dragon of the land of what became Wales[44], while the white dragon is of a foreign land. Instead of a saint who pacifies them, it is a boy, Myrddin, born of a human mother and a father from the otherworld. He tells the king of their presence, who then uncovers the underground lake and their prison. The two dragons, once released, fight each other and then eventually return to their own homes, the red dragon back underground and the white dragon to a land across the sea.

44. This is the reason for the red dragon on the flag of Wales

From this tale, we see a clear connection between dragons and land (and as in Coulobre and Graoully with rivers and subterranean water), which provides the key to these other dragon stories in Celtic lands. Likewise, the fact that these stories are so prevalent in Christian hagiography[45] and conversion narratives of the Celtic peoples points to the sacred nature of such beings.

Celtic stories of dragons appear not very different from the Shinto animist beliefs about dragons, especially in that so many are related to water and rivers. In Shinto, dragons are a kind of *kami*, a spirit which can be either a god, a force of nature such as wind or rain, a specific place, an object (like a tree or rock), an ancestor, natural principles such as growth, or a guardian.

In Shinto belief, a *kami* is both invisible yet also obvious and evident, because their presence evokes a human response. European Pagan and animist beliefs appear to have been similar: a place itself was inhabited by a spirit, a spirit who was not actually separate from the place but actually also part of the place. The dragon Coulobre, for example, she of the massive and awe-inspiring Fountain of Vaucluse, was both an inhabitant of the place and also the place itself, just as the Tarasque and the place where it lived (now called Tarascon) seem to have been related and inseparable.

45. "The stories of saints." A remarkable amount of knowledge regarding Pagan gods can be gleaned from such stories, as often these stories are clear attempts to convert Pagans to Christianity by assimilating their stories into Catholic doctrine. For instance, the Catholic stories of Saint Brigid are clear and blatant retellings of the stories of the goddess Brigid.

Often with these dragon stories there are hints or even clear evidence of religious veneration on those sites. For instance, the massive pool of the Vaucluse has been found to be full of ancient coin offerings, and a druid grove was is said to have been cut down near the spring and a church was built over it.

THE MATTER OF THE GIANTS

Another sacred place points us to a link between land, dragons, and also to gods in the ancient animist belief of the Celts. The famous Mont St. Michel, a monastic complex built upon a tidal island off the coast of Normandy, bears several depictions of the Archangel Michael slaying a dragon. Yet no dragon stories were known to be associated with the mount, but rather two other stories, that of a giant (named Garguntua, from which our English word "gargantuan" is derived) and of a god, Belenos.

Giants in many of the later Welsh and Irish recordings of Pagan stories are often associated with gods. For instance the god Brân, whose name means raven, was said to be a giant so large "no house could hold him." Irish gods such as the Dagda were also said to be giants, and in the Arthurian legends we see the same thing happening to giants as to dragons: Arthur kills them or drives them off in order to establish his Christian kingdom.

While dragons are less common in Germanic, Slavic, and other peoples further to the east, giants very often appear, both as directly related to places or to natural formations (as for example mountain giants) or in the figures of Norse Jötnar. Here, though, we need to speak about the term "giant" itself, which while it now just refers to something large, originally referred to a group of beings in Greek Paganism called the Gigantes (thus "gigantic").

The Gigantes were said to be the children of Gaia, born of the earth herself, and were the untamed spirits of natural forces such as wind, volcanic eruptions, storms, and others. They were not necessarily large beings (some were), but because of a translation error by an early Christian, the word "giant" then became used for the Nephilim (the offspring of certain angels and human women, who were said to be massive people), thus causing giant to then always mean "tall" in English.

In fact, the Norse Jötnar were not necessarily thought to always be tall or massive either. Jötnar means "devourer," and the other word used for them, *þursar* (pronounced "thursar") means "powerful," rather than tall or massive.

The giants in the Arthurian legends, the giants in Welsh and Irish pagan stories, the Gigantes of the Greek Pagans, and the countless stories of dragons all appear to have one striking thing in common: they are all associated with nature itself, whether that is a specific place of land or water, or with a natural force such as earthquakes, storms, and floods. Here we can see that the ancient animist ideas in Shinto about the *kami* seems to describe the same group: a class of spirits that come from nature or are expressions of nature itself.

Another parallel that we can draw between these indigenous animist beliefs in Europe and the animism of Shinto is that the dividing lines between what is a god, what is a land spirit, what is an ancestor, and what is a force of nature are not really lines at all. In Norse and Germanic beliefs, the landvættir (land spirits or land wights) are sometimes giants, sometimes elves, sometimes dwarves, and sometimes the spirits of humans or completely impersonal spirits. This has a parallel in many of the Celtic ideas of the faeries, who are not at all the tiny winged beings that modern myth depicts them as. The Korrigan, for example, who are the Breton (a Celtic people in Northwest France) faeries, are actually thought to be the souls of the dead who have become land spirits. The Korrigan are said to fiercely guard old standing stones, alignments, and tombs, killing those who trespass at the wrong time of day.

In both the Welsh lore and also the Germanic lore, giants are sometimes ferociously violent and sometimes kind guardians of knowledge, and sometimes they are gods themselves. For example, the Welsh god Brân was a giant, and was also in the possession of a gift given him by giants who fled from Ireland, a cauldron from the underworld of which they were the guardians. That cauldron was said to return the dead back to life, but those who entered it would not ever speak. Other such cauldrons were held by other giants, and in the

Arthurian legends, Arthur slays the giants in order to gain possession of the cauldrons.[46]

In Norse lore, though the Jötnar are the "enemies" of the gods, many of the gods themselves were descended at least partially from such beings (and Loki was himself a child of two Jötnar). There are two groups of gods in Norse lore, the Æsir and the Vanir, and that second group, which includes the goddess Freyja and the gods Frey and Njord, appear to occupy a similar category of "earthly" beings as the Greek Gigantes and Irish Fomhoire. They are all "older" gods, all associated with the earth, earthly places, natural forces, and the most basic aspects of life and human interactions with the world around them.

Such gods, spirits, and other beings are usually referred to as "chthonic," which has taken on the sense of "underworld" or the realms of the dead. However, chthonic in its original Greek (*khthon*) referred specifically to what lived within the earth, with the sense of the roots of a tree being within (rather than just "under.") Chthonic beings include ancestors and the dead (because their bodies are put within the earth), but all other spirits that emanate from the buried or hidden aspects of the earth and nature.

This same word, chthonic, came later to also refer to gods of older societies or inhabitants of a place (such as the Fomhoire

---

46. The Celtic ideas regarding cauldrons are deeply fascinating. Ceridwen is said to have brewed a potion of divine inspiration in a cauldron (the Cauldron of Awen). The Dagda (a giant god of the Irish) possessed a cauldron which was always full of food. But also natural places are referred to as cauldrons, which leads to the possibility that cauldrons are themselves a kind of power or spirit of the land.

and the Vanir) who were inherited by later peoples and still recognised. Hecate is one such chthonic goddess and Saturn is one such chthonic god, beings worshiped and revered by people in the lands that later became Greece or Rome.

Put another way, they were gods of the land itself, gods who were within the land and therefore needed to be recognised by later Pagan peoples regardless of their other gods. In many cases, chthonic gods were also ancestors of other gods: for instance, the Celtic god Lugh is said in Irish lore to have been mothered or foster-mothered by one of the Fomhoire, the goddess (and likely giantess) Tailtu.

Tailtu is said to have been the mother of farming for the Irish Celts, having tilled all the land herself so that her foster-son and his people could survive. In this story we see another interesting aspect of many of the chthonic gods, as they are often associated with the earliest forms of farming, of settlements, and of providing for people. Freyj, the Vanir goddess of the Norse and also the Germanic peoples (who called her Frey), is a chthonic goddess of fertility and abundance, as well as domestic life, the hearth, and magic.

A GOD? A LANDSPIRIT? OR BOTH?

This apparent mixing of groups of gods reflects something we can easily forget about the ancient world: people traveled and intermixed. The lines between gods and other spirits is often blurry, and also the lineage of the gods is often very mixed, but this is also true of the people who knew these gods.

As mentioned, the Vanir gods (such as Freyja) were a different sort of god from the Æsir (such as Odin). But of course, Odin and Freyj married, and Odin himself had giant lineage, as did others of the Æsir. Yet the Æsir and Vanir were said to have been once at war, just as the Jötnar are still at war with the Æsir up to the foretold end of Ragnorok.

While even many who take these stories seriously and recognise the existence of these gods tend to dismiss these lineages as mere details in the lore, the parallels of this sort of intermixing in other Pagan lore (Celtic and Greek especially) points to actual changes in people groups. The Vanir, being gods closer to the "chthonic" types of gods and spirits, were likely local gods or spirits of places and of the land itself. That is, they represented a more organic and direct kind of relationship to gods and spirits through the land, while the Æsir appear to be more gods or spirits of communities or people groups.

Freyja is a fascinating example of this, and one personally interesting to me as she is one of the gods I recognise in my twice daily rituals. Not far from where I live is a natural rock formation upon which is carved two figures. The site appears to have been a place of ritual and worship, and it is not far from the ruins of an ancient Celtic town (an *oppidum*).

The place is now called Freyley, meaning "Freyja's Rocks." However, the Celtic oppidum and the ritual use of the site pre-dates the coming of Germanic peoples here, meaning that it is highly unlikely the Treveri (the Celtic people who were here before them) worshipped Freyja there. Unfortunately, there is no other evidence or record of who the Treveri revered there, but another site much farther north, as well as the legend of a Christian saint, provides an answer.

In what is now Belgium, there was until the 6th century a stone statue of a huntress woman whom the people worshipped. St. Walfroy, a Christian bishop intent upon converting the local peoples, railed against the worship of the woman and, in one story, supposedly sat on a tall pole nearby, threatening never to come down unless the statue was also torn down. A later writer, Gregory of Tours, states that this statue was of "Diana," but all the evidence instead points to it being of the goddess Arduinna.

Arduinna is both the name of a goddess and also the name of the forests where she was worshipped, something seen quite often in Gaul and other Celtic lands. That forest, which is called now the Ardennes, once covered all of what is now Belgium, Luxembourg, must of north-eastern France, and the parts of Germany called the Rhineland-Palitanate. Thus, the worship of a huntress goddess in one part of the forest was likely also linked to the worship of a huntress goddess in other parts of the forest. So, besides being attested to in Latin religious inscriptions in the area, there are even later examples of a cult to Arduinna, up to the 11th century, which the Christian church complained about.

So, it is a great likelihood that this spot near my home was used to venerate Arduinna before becoming a site of worship of Freyja (and thus later named Freyley). Here, though Arduinna was a Celtic goddess and Freyja a goddess of the Germanic peoples, the transition from the worship of one to the other in such sites can't really be said to be much of a transition at all. Arduinna was both a forest goddess and a goddess of hunting; while Frejya is not directly associated with either, she has a boar companion whom she was said to also ride, linking her to statues thought to be likely of Arduinna also riding or accompanied by a boar.

Are Arduinna and Freyja therefore the same being? No, but this is the wrong and overly modern question. Consider a different question instead: where does a forest end, and where does it begin?

The Ardennes forest once covered all of this area, yet now most of the forest has been cut down or is otherwise divided by roads. The forest where the Freyley stands is no longer connected to the other parts of the forest, yet it once was. Is it still correct to call that forest the Ardennes? During much of the Roman Empire and long before, the Ardennes forest was once part of a much larger forest, the Hercynian forest, which covered much of Europe, extending from the westernmost parts of France to eastern parts of Poland. Is it really true, then, to say that the Ardennes was a separate forest from the Black Forest, the Morvenne, the Vosges, and any of the other forests it was once part of?

In the same way that it is not possible to really define the borders of a forest, it is not possible to define the boundaries of people and cultures. When the Germanic Frankish people moved into the lands of the Treveri who previously lived here, the Treveri didn't disappear, nor did their culture. The Franks and the Treveri married each other, lived amongst each other, and the result was a culture that did not look fully Germanic nor fully Celtic.

The same can be said of all the migrations of peoples throughout Europe, but also the same is true of those in Africa, in Asia, and also in the Americas pre-colonization. When one group arrives, the other group doesn't just go away. Even if that new group is more dominant, the resulting culture is a reflection of both.

For a fascinating example of this, consider the complicated history of the language I am writing this in, English. English is a mix of Germanic and Romance languages. The Angles and the Saxons were both Germanic peoples who settled in Britain and intermixed with the Celtic peoples who were already there, and the language they spoke up until the year 1066 was a melange of those three currents. In 1066, the French-speaking Normans (who were themselves a mix of Celtic and Norse peoples) invaded Britain, and the addition of their language and culture to what was already there created the English language. Also, ironically, French means *Frankish* (the Germanic peoples previously mentioned), but the French don't speak Frankish but rather a language derived from

Latin, which was one of the indigenous languages from Italy[47] that later became the official language of the Roman Empire.

So, just a forest cannot easily be defined, people groups cannot be easily defined or divided into discrete categories. The same is true of the gods those people revered and knew, as well as their rituals and customs involving those gods. Likewise, just as it is not true to say English is also German, it is not true to say that Freyja is also Arduinna. Nor is it possible to truly say English is a language completely separate from German or from French, and thus we also cannot truly say Freyja and Arduinna are completely separate, either.

Another thing to note in the case of many gods such as Arduinna is that there is no clear division between the god as a separate being and the place they are worshiped or associated with. Goddesses of rivers are often both a goddess of those rivers and also the river itself, such as spirits of trees or springs are both spirits independent of the spring but also indivisible from the spring. In the words of G.K. Chesterton, "the old Greeks could not see the trees for the dryads," meaning that for Pagans, there was little difference between the spirit of the thing and the thing itself.

47. And to add something even more interesting to this, the Italic Tribes (the peoples of Italy before the founding of Rome) have shared ancestors with the Celts and the Germanic peoples, and Latin shares some similar language forms to Celtic ones. Additionally, Celtic peoples lived in on the Italian peninsula alongside the Etruscans and Latins, so Latin absolutely had Celtic influences.

WHAT TO DO ABOUT THE GODS

So, now we can return to our original questions: what exactly is a god? What exactly is a spirit? But by now, you've probably also understood that this question cannot be answered in the way it was asked, because it was the wrong question.

Still, we can try to answer it by looking at what ancient peoples wrote about them, especially the Greeks. However, in such writing we find that they don't really know either; rather, they seem as perplexed about the matter as any of us might be now. What they are not perplexed about, however, is that there are gods at all.

Put another way, ancient peoples took gods and spirits as a given the way we now take wind, rain, and storms as a given. We know such things exist, but unless we are a sailor, a farmer, or a meteorologist, we rarely actually think about them except when the wind, the rain, or a storm is particularly strong and affecting us directly.

Pagan peoples appear to have looked at the gods and spirits in the same way. Priests, druids, shamans, oracles, mystics, and poets gave their time in contemplation of such things, but the majority of others only ever thought about the gods or spirits when there was a problem, or they had particularly profound or disturbing dreams, desired a blessing for something they were about to do, or needed help with something they could not resolve on their own.

At most, the "average" person tended a small shrine in the home, or visited shrines to ancestors on special days, or made prayers or offerings to a god a few times a year, and participated in community rituals that were often also festivals. In such rituals, the religious significance of the event blended seamlessly with the cultural entertainment aspects like drinking, feasting, and meeting potential sexual mates.

That is, the existence of gods and spirits was part of the cultural fabric of life itself, rather than a question to be complicated or a philosophical matter to be unraveled. This has parallels to the way the Catholic churches in small European villages historically (and sometimes still) functioned not just as a religious building, but also as the centre of village life, as a place of meeting, of celebration, and a place for many of the other activities that compose community.

This is the way also that the *kami* are seen in Shinto, the way the gods are seen in Hinduism, and the way gods and spirits were treated in African animist religions as well. Some people become priests and tend the shrines of gods and spirits, but the vast majority of people do not become priests and only occasionally visit such shrines.

Such priests have a kind of role in their societies that is a bit difficult for us moderns to fully understand, and one that is deeply different from the role of a Catholic priest. While both kinds of priests act as interpreters between people and the gods and spirits, the role of the priest in Pagan, animist societies is also to make sure the gods and spirits are pleased, lest they wreak havoc.

This role can be best seen in many African animist societies, in which long rituals are performed by priests and the kings or chiefs together to make sure that the gods stay "in their place." Sometimes, these rituals actually involve chasing gods or spirits out of a community, a home, or even a person, or bribing these beings with offerings or promises so that they will not disrupt everyday life.

While it might be tempting to think of this as parallel to the Christian idea of a "vengeful god," it's actually closer to a Catholic exorcism rite. However, in those rites a demon who is wreaking havoc on a human is bound and chased out; in Pagan cultures, the spirits are not seen as "evil" or "fallen" but rather just in the wrong place for a reason that needs to be understood and resolved.

Here we can look at two practices that are widespread throughout many Pagan cultures: rituals of ancestral remembrance and rituals to hearth or home spirits. Lighting candles or tending a shrine to ancestors is both an act of reverence to them but also an act of making sure they are pleased. That is, it is an act of honour in the sense of its older English meaning: giving respect to and also welcoming as a guest. Or put another way, it is an act of hospitality, a concept deeply important in countless pagan societies throughout the ancient world.

Giving hospitality to a guest in ancient societies involved much more than giving them food or drink. Rather, it was an act of mutual obligation on both the part of the guest and the host, both of which agreed to exchange something with each other through the relationship of hospitality. That exchange was rarely financial or material, but rather a sense of continued obligation on the part of the guest, who would always then seek the best for their host, "returning the favour."

The word *favour* comes from Latin *favorem*, meaning kindness, inclination, partiality, or support. To favour someone was to support them or think of them with good will, to be on their side. So in hospitality, in exchange for being favoured by the host, a guest thus agrees to later favour the host. Such favour could of course mean merely also hosting at another time, but could also just as often mean physically protecting the host against enemies or arguing in their defence against those who wish that person ill.

So, in ancestral veneration, a person is showing a favour to the ancestors and returning favour that those ancestors showed to them. It is a reciprocal relationship between the person and the ancestors, one that continues to benefit both the living and the dead.

The second widespread practice, that of creating shrines for hearth or home spirits, is also an act of hospitality. By setting aside a place for such a spirit in a home, they are welcomed into the home in the way a guest would be welcomed, with the literal sense of the words "make yourself at home."

Stories of helpful house spirits are particularly abundant in Celtic and German lore, many of which have survived through fairy tales that we still learn today. For instance, the story of the shoemaker and the elves, in which an old shoemaker wakes each morning to find his work completed mysteriously in the night, is a such a tale. Those elves have a name, the *heinzelmännchen*, and they were said even to have helped build cathedrals for overworked masons.

One of the most common aspects of such stories, incidentally, is that such beings appreciate only a tiny bit of attention but not more. In fact, too much attention makes them go away, just as giving them no attention will make them leave. Thus, shrines to house spirits were often very simple affairs, and offerings to them were quite simple (a small bowl of milk, for example, or the bit ends of cakes or breads). There seems to be an importance in acknowledging them in subtle and very sideways manners, more like they are neighbours rather than family members.

In fact, "neighbour" is probably the best way for a modern to understand the Pagan relationship between humans and gods and spirits. A neighbour is literally someone who lives nearby, someone whose life and existence is related to yours but not a direct part of yours. The gods and spirits have their own lives and own worlds, just as we do. But we live next door to each other, and just as the lives of our neighbours affect us usually in very subtle ways but sometimes in profound ways, it is the same for the gods, the spirits, and the humans who are each others' neighbours.

THE OTHER

Beyond the belief in gods and spirits, another core aspect of the Pagan, animist, and indigenous framework throughout the world and throughout history is the belief in some form of magic.

For modern people, whose worldview is dominated by the concept of reason and the mistaken belief that we have "progressed" to a more advanced (and therefore "superior" or "true") way of seeing the world, this can be an incredibly difficult thing to comprehend. We believe ourselves to live in an age defined by scientific knowledge, of rational thinking, to have transcended the superstitious and "primitive" beliefs of earlier people. Therefore, the very notion that magic might exist is quickly dismissed.

Yet despite this, interest in magic and the occult has always permeated this "secular" modern order. Horoscopes can be found in almost every newspaper, and journals such as *The Atlantic* and *The New York Times* have published many articles in the last few years remarking on a dramatic increase in interest for witchcraft and new age healing practices.[48]

Interest in the occult and magic isn't just recent. For instance, the two best selling non-religious texts—in any language—in all of human history both prominently feature magic: *The Hobbit*, by J.R.R. Tolkien (140.6 million copies) and *Harry Potter and The Philosopher's Stone* by J.K. Rowling (120 million copies).[49]

Books are not the only place where the persistence of occult and magical interest can be seen. Throughout the 19th and 20th centuries, esoteric movements sprung up throughout Europe, blending occult themes and Pagan ideas together into new forms. Spiritualism (and its related movement, Spiritism) were both formed in the middle of the 1800's around the idea that certain humans could contact angels, demons, and the dead. A little later in England, the Hermetic Order of the Golden Dawn arose as a secret society dedicated to the pursuit of ritual magic and occult knowledge. At almost the same time, the Theosophical Society was founded in the United States by a Russian esotericist, Helena Blavatsky.

Those two movements greatly influenced the thinking of three famous occultists who have shaped the way many people now look at magic and the occult: Gerald Gardner, Doreen

48 For instance, "When Did Everyone Become a Witch" in *The New York Times* (2019), "Why Is Witchcraft On the Rise" in *The Atlantic* (2020)

49. In fact, half of the top 20 selling books of all time in any language feature magic. Seven of these are by the same author, J.K. Rowling.

Valiente, and Aleister Crowley. Gerald Gardner and Doreen Valiente co-created a new religious movement called Wicca, which has now become wrongly seen as synonymous with witchcraft and Paganism both, while Aleister Crowley founded the occult tradition Thelema.

We can look even earlier than this, into "The Enlightenment" itself, to see that interest in the occult permeated the thoughts and writing even of the founders of rationalism. Isaac Newton, for instance, wrote extensively on alchemy and angels, while Francis Bacon, "the founder of empiricism," was actively involved as a jurist against accused witches in England. Jean Bodin, whose *Six Books On the Commonwealth* are the political foundation for the modern, secular nation-state, also wrote a study of demons and the occult. And of course, just a little earlier, there were the famous Renaissance magicians, whose works form the foundation of many alchemical, astrological, and goetic practices today.

THE NATURE OF MAGIC

Though there has absolutely been a persistent fascination with magic and the occult throughout the last half a millennium, and though many of the architects of our modern secular framework were themselves deeply studied in such subjects, our current conception of magic is quite warped and bears little resemblance to theirs, let alone the more ancient and widespread Pagan conception.

While writing about magic and the occult thus far, I have been particularly careful to avoid a certain word whose absence you may have noticed: "supernatural." The reason for this is because, in a Pagan framework, *there is no such thing.*

That doesn't mean that Pagan, animist, and indigenous peoples have no concept of magic. On the contrary, magic forms a core part of their understanding of the world. Similar to their understanding of gods and spirits, however, magic is not a supernatural process or act for them, but rather *a fully natural one.* That is, just as gods and spirits are part of the natural world, so too is magic.

Believing magic to be part of the natural world is very similar to believing the body to be inseparable from a human. Just as our modern alienation from the body often leads us to see our minds as outside the body or the body as something external to us, our modern misunderstanding of nature leads us to assume that magic, spirits, and the gods must be external to it.

Our alienation from body is an important obstacle to our understanding of magic, so we need to explore this problem again. Here, Silvia Federici's previously cited essay, "In Praise of the Dancing Body," is yet even more useful:

> What we have not always seen is what the separation from the land and nature has meant for our body, which has been pauperized and stripped of the powers that pre-capitalist populations attributed to it.
>
> Nature has been inorganic body and there was a time when we could read the winds, the clouds, and the changes

in the currents of rivers and seas. In pre-capitalist societies people thought they had the power to fly, to have out-of body experiences, to communicate, to speak with animals and take on their powers and even shape-shift. They also thought that they could be in more places than one and, for example, they could come back from the grave to take revenge of their enemies.

Not all these powers were imaginary. Daily contact with nature was the source of a great amount of knowledge reflected in the food revolution that took place especially in the Americas prior to colonization or in the revolution in sailing techniques. We know now, for instance, that the Polynesian populations used to travel the high seas at night with only their body as their compass, as they could tell from the vibrations of the waves the different ways to direct their boats to the shore. [50]

Here, Silvia Federici offers a tantalising look at something that very few other writers have explored. The ability to feel by the vibrations of waves how far your boat is from land sounds like a "supernatural" power, yet it is something quite natural and something that the body is capable of doing.

Here we can remember what I wrote about when we spoke of the moon, that I can know without looking or consulting any external chart where it will rise and in what phase it will be. This, to someone who has never thought on such things or who has not made a habit of looking at the moon, could easily seem "supernatural," but it's actually a fully natural thing to be able to do.

50. Federici, S. (2016, August 22). In Praise Of The Dancing Body. A Beautiful Resistance. https://abeautifulresistance.org/site/2016/08/22/in-praise-of-the-dancing-body

There are countless other such acts and perceptions which are seen by some as supernatural but are instead abilities of the body we have forgotten in our modern world. That is, they are all quite natural abilities, but our modern definition of what is natural has become too small and limited.

A peculiar phenomenon known as "blindsight" illustrates this quite well. In blindsight, people whose visual cortex (the part of the brain responsible for translating light stimuli into images) has been irreversibly damaged (and are therefore completely blind) still are able to judge distances, point out the direction of bright lights or objects, and even correctly notice when someone is looking directly at them.[51]

A blind person shouldn't be able to do those tasks, of course, since such things are thought to be only possible with sight. However, they can, and this has led "rational" re-searchers to come to a conclusion that is remarkably similar to the supposedly irrational animist one: *our consciousness is not our only source of knowledge.* Instead, there are unconscious processes and sensations to which our bodies are constantly reacting which we rarely ever notice.

51. Robson, D. (2015, September 25). Blindsight: the strangest form of consciousness. BBC Future. https://www.bbc.com/future/article/20150925-blindsight-the-strangest-form-of-consciousness

THE UNCONSCIOUS AND THE CONSCIOUS

Consider that feeling you have when someone else is in the room with you that you didn't expect, and then suddenly you notice they are really there. Before you were consciously aware of their presence, you were unconsciously aware of them. That is, there was a bodily awareness before there was a mental awareness.

When we speak of unconscious, then, what we really mean is everything that the body knows and senses. What is conscious, therefore, is only the part of the knowledge and sensation that has our immediate attention.

There's a rather funny trick I like to show my friends and my partner which often will both amaze and terrify them. When I am cooking and in the process of chopping vegetables with a very sharp knife, I will talk directly to them while looking completely away from the knife and from what I am cutting. Once they notice that I am not actually paying attention to what I am doing, their response is usually one of panic: "you'll cut yourself!" they'll warn.

I don't actually cut myself though, because I have learned to slice things very accurately by only touch. This is what some call "body memory," the same kind of process by which you can find your way through a dark room that you know very well or type without looking at a keyboard or at the screen.

"Body memory" is a kind of unconscious knowledge, just as blindsight is. In blindsight, the body of a blind person still senses distance and directed attention because such knowledge is coming through the body itself, regardless of whether or not the body informs their conscious perception.

Consider all the daily activities you perform without ever focusing on them, and you will begin to get a sense of how truly vast the body's capabilities really are. Walking, for example: you move throughout the world with legs accurately stepping flatly on the earth without ever once losing your balance and toppling over. This is an unconscious skill, an act of the body that rarely requires your direct attention. You daily chew and digest food and drink water without choking or drowning yourself, and never once need to direct the act of swallowing. You probably dress without actually thinking about putting on each article of clothing, perhaps only ever giving attention to which clothes you will wear that day. If like me you ride a bike, you are engaging in a completely unconscious and quite astounding act of keeping yourself upright on two wheels, only directing your conscious thoughts to where you're riding and to avoid obstacles or cars.

Very few of these things which the body does ever have our attention or focus, and that is probably for the best. In fact, often consciousness will get in the way of many of the things we need to do. If you think too hard about riding a bike and try to control the movements of balance, you are likely to fall. When you dance, focusing too much on the steps will make you miss them. Likewise, if you try to go to sleep you are quite likely instead to find yourself wide awake, just as trying to direct the slicing of vegetables with conscious effort is likely to result in cutting yourself.[52]

The body knows things we don't ever think about or even realize we know. Since we are our bodies, what I really mean here is that *we know things we don't realize we know.*

MAGIC AND THE BODY

Here we can look again at the question of magic. One of the definitions of magic, put forward by Aleister Crowley, is that it is the "science and art of causing change to occur in conformity to will." A more Pagan definition, however, would be "aligning consciousness to the body in order to enact change."

That is to say, we moderns have it all wrong: the body is not the servant of the mind, but rather consciousness is the servant of the body. Consciousness, or "the mind," are not the "real us," but rather just one part of us. Consciousness is the directed gaze of the body, where the body looks and what the body chooses to give attention to. That gaze is not possible without the body, in the same way eyes cannot see when they are removed from the body.

Aligning our consciousness to the knowledge of the body means, at the very basic level, giving attention to what the

---

52. This goes for many, many other things. For instance, stuttering is often cured by helping the person stop giving attention to the act of speaking, and sexual dysfunction is usually cured in people by training them to stop thinking about the sex act.

body is telling us. As mentioned in the chapter on the body, often times experiences of anxiety, depression, panic, or despair are actually our consciousness misinterpreting bodily sensations. Are we really depressed, or are we actually tired? Are we really anxious, or are we actually hungry? Is there really a reason to despair, or have we just not taken a deep breath for awhile nor had a drink of water?

Learning to tell the difference here is crucial not just for our own health and sanity, but also for performing any sort of magic. Consider: if your consciousness is constantly misinterpreting core bodily sensations such as hunger, thirst, and fatigue, how much more would it misinterpret more complex and much more rare sensations, such as the presence of a god or spirit?

That is, to align consciousness with the body in order to enact change, we must first understand what the body is already saying. Many religious and esoteric traditions recommend meditation for this kind of work, which can be useful but is hardly the only or even necessarily best way to do this. In most forms of meditation, a person "stills" their thoughts in order to have better control over the consciousness and the ways it is directed. In forms of mediation that I have found much more useful, the focus is not so much on quieting thoughts but rather being aware of how those thoughts relate to sensations of the body.

In these other forms, when a thought arises, you direct your consciousness towards where that thought might be located in the body. The goal here is to approach these thoughts and their relationship to bodily sensations with a sense of curiosity, rather than judgment. For example, the thought *I'm bored* might correspond to stress in your lower back or legs, perhaps a subtle pain or exhaustion of those muscles. In such a case, the body desires to shift or move to release that tension, and boredom (which is really just wanting to do something else) is how this desire is consciously translated.[53]

Practicing these latter forms of meditation are one way of aligning your consciousness to body, but there are many more active ways of doing this as well. For instance, weight training, hard exercise, and martial arts all lead to such an alignment, because in all such training our conscious attention is pulled into a sense of immediacy through the intensity of bodily sensations. When I do leg presses at the gym for instance, an exercise that requires pushing several hundred pounds of weight with just the muscles of the legs, my consciousness can only focus on what the body is doing and what the physical sensations are. Here, the mind must listen precisely to what those sensations are, determining when the levels of pain are healthy and useful (all weight training damages muscle tissue, which is how muscles grow) and when the pain indicates a joint or tendon might snap. In many martial arts, conscious awareness is trained to "follow" the body,

---

53 This is a deeply crucial insight for anyone who wishes to practice magic. The body experiences things our consciousness constantly attempts to translate, and often times the translation is wrong. However, through practice, you can begin to correct those translations in your conscious thought so that you understand better what is being experienced and can discern what is coming from "normal" sensations and what is coming from an external influence.

rather than direct the body, since it is the body rather than our conscious attention that senses where an opponent is about to strike and what movement is required to counter or avoid that strike.

Martial arts are also useful in developing a wider field of sensation than what our conscious attention normally acknowledges. An esoteric way of describing this is "extending the subtle body," with the subtle body meaning the field of sensation that extends beyond the apparent physical body itself.

One need not train in martial arts (though it is profoundly useful) to develop this, however. Here, other physical activities like dancing are helpful. Some recommend consuming entheogenic substances,[54] and this can be a useful path for some. I would be remiss if I did not admit I myself used quite a few such aids several decades ago, but I also do not think they are necessary. The same altered states they create are all possible to attain without their use.[55]

54. Substances that temporarily alter perception or consciousness, such as hallucinogenic mushrooms, or the wide array of plants used ritually by indigenous people.

55. For instance, many of these altered states can be created through controlling breath rhythms either through hyperventilation (breathing very rapidly) or slowing your rate of breathing to the bare minimum. It is absolutely safest at the beginning to be guided through these practices by another person, just as for the use of entheogens.

INTUITION, INSIGHT, INSPIRATION, & CHARISMA

All of these practices to align your consciousness with your body ultimately lead to a deeper connection to what is often called *intuition*. Intuition comes from Latin and has a Pagan root sense. The core root of intuition is also the root word of the word tutor: *tueri*, which meant "to watch over" or "to guard." Thus, intuition is a kind of inner tutor or guardian, something (or someone) watching over you from within.

This idea of intuition being an inner guardian is a deeply Pagan idea, found especially in Greek and Roman Pagan beliefs. The Greeks recognised a being called *eudaemon*, a kind of benevolent spirit that would protect and watch over particular humans. Plato recounts how Socrates claimed to have such an *eudaemon* since childhood who often whispered warnings to him. Roman Pagans spoke of and often made shrines to the *genii*,[56] personal attendant spirits that are with people from the moment of their births to the moment of their deaths[57] and are to some degree also a part of the person.

56. Though this word looks remarkably similar to the Arabic word for spirits, *djen* (or *djinni*) which was translated as "genie" in English, etymologists believe they are completely unrelated.

57. These two Pagan concepts were later borrowed by Saint Augustine and became folded into the Christian concept of the "eternal soul," though this is absolutely not their original meaning. The folk Christian belief in guardian angels, however, is a much closer approximation (and technically a Pagan continuation) of the original ideas.

Both the *eudaemon* and the *genius*[58] were spirits independent from a person, yet were also seen as somewhat inseparable from the person themselves. Rather than being a paradox, though, this points to something profound about the Pagan view of spirits, intelligence, and the nature of thought itself.

This can be seen in another Latin-derived English word that we often use when describing a kind of inner and rare knowledge: *inspiration*, which comes from the same root as the words respiration and spirit. To be inspired was to have breathed something in, or to have a spirit inside you.

This link between spirits and breath is not just a Latin one: our word *ghost* comes from the Germanic-derived old English word *gast*, which could equally refer to a spirit, an angel, a demon, a breath, or a man.[59] And in Greek, the word for spirit is the same word for breath and breathing, *pneuma*.[60]

This link between breathing and spirits answers the apparent paradox of the *eudaemon* and the *genius* being both independent yet also inseparable from a person, because of the principle of interpenetration. As Kadmus notes in *True to the Earth:*

> There is another aspect of the gods we haven't talked
> about yet, namely the way they can inspire, be channeled by,

58. The singular of the plural *genii*, which is also the source of our modern English usage of genius, meaning someone with a particularly rare kind of insight.

59. The word *wight*, which usually only refers now to a kind of undead, also originally could refer to a man, a thing, or a demon.

60. This is the root of the words pneumatic and pneumonia, and also the French word for tires, *pneu*, referencing the fact they are filled with air.

or even possess humans. In Pagan cultures when a person embodies a particularly striking characteristic that falls within the domain of a given god, they were frequently understood to have become that god. Sometimes, this is described as the god appearing as the person. Sometimes, the god is described as inspiring or dictating the actions of the person (for example, Athena talking to Odysseus to guide his wisdom while no one else sees or hears her). Sometimes, the god is said to directly enter and possess the person. All of these are attested to in Ancient Greek literature, but nowhere is there a more highly developed expertise on the varieties of relations like these than in African traditional and diasporic religions.

This aspect of the embodied gods makes clear that gods and the rest of the entities that make up the cosmos (especially humanity) are really inter-bodied. We flow in and out of each other, as interweaving ongoing events which mutually define us. Understanding bodies as matrices of relational actions and events helps us to understand how the bodies of the gods can go through the many changes that they do, as well as being able to interpenetrate our own. [61]

Consider the act of breathing. When we inhale, we pull in oxygen which circulates through our blood. When we exhale, we release carbon dioxide that the body creates through all its life activities. So then, is the air we breathe actually an internal or external part of the body? The answer of course is that it is both.

This is the key to the Pagan understanding of spirits and also that of consciousness, insight, and inspiration. The *genius* and the *eudaemon* are both internal and external to us

61. Kadmus. (2018). *True To The Earth*. Gods&Radicals Press

because they flow in and out of us the way air flows in and out. Sometimes we have particular flashes of "genius" and are said to be "inspired," and sometimes we escape particular harm through apparent chance or the "gut feeling" of intuition that to others—and also to ourselves—may look like someone or something was watching over us.

In our modern framework the conclusion when such things occur is that a person is merely "fortunate" or is particularly "gifted." Both of these ways of looking at the world actually contain one half of the Pagan conception. Consider: to be gifted implies that there was *someone who gave the gift*. Luck and fortune both derive from Pagan concepts implying the same relationship: they were things *given* to someone by the gods, rather than just random acts of chance.[62]

One last concept, this time from the Greek, can help further explain the Pagan way of understanding intuition and inspiration, as well as the relationship between our conscious attention and the body of knowledge we call the unconscious. As Kadmus noted in the section I cited above, when someone appeared to do something strikingly powerful, or to be particularly beautiful, or to possess some unique and renowned trait that others were drawn to, Pagan peoples saw the presence or the influence of a god in that person. The Greek word for this was *kharisma*, meaning "divine favour or gift."

A person with *kharisma* (or charisma, as we now spell it) was seen as having been touched or gifted by a god who favoured

---

62. Chance comes from Latin *cadentia*, which meant "what fell out," referring to how dice fell out of hands or a cup when thrown.

them. A god of beauty, for example, might have gifted a person with particularly stunning beauty, just as a god of wisdom might have given a gift of divine insight to another. Crucial to this was that everyone around the person immediately recognised the presence of such a gift and connected the gift to a divine giver.

Charisma is a concept which remains in modern secular society still, though we usually see it as a dangerous trait. A charismatic person seems to have an uncanny power of drawing people to them through charm,[63] or their beauty, or just a "magnetic personality," and many times such people are seen as potentially destructive (for instance, a charismatic cult leader or politician). Even in this negative view, however, we can detect a continuation of the Pagan idea that behind such unique and alluring traits was a powerful influence that could not easily be reckoned with.

Here we can see how our concept of genius now also still continues some degree of this Pagan framework. A person who is a genius is thought to be profoundly intelligent or to possess a very rare and powerful degree of insight or intuition about a situation. For the Pagans, such people were not geniuses themselves, but had particularly helpful *genii* to whom they listened.

---

63. Again from Latin, charm originally referred to a specific kind of song used in religious rites, an incantation. *Enchant* has the same root.

LISTENING TO THE OTHER

This is the key to this Pagan framework of magic, of aligning consciousness to the unconscious in order to affect change. A person could be surrounded by all the helpful spirits in the world, but if they did not listen to them then their life would be one misfortune after another. Similarly, a person could have a particularly insightful *genius* constantly alerting them to danger or offering them insight into the world around them, but if that person did not listen then none of it amounts to anything.

What we call the unconscious is the body and all that the information the body constantly attempts to convey. Whether that information is simply hunger and thirst or intuitive glimpses and strokes of genius and inspiration, it is all worthless if we insist that our conscious attention—our minds, or what Freud called the *ego*—is the true seat of knowledge.

Once we recognise the unconscious for what it is, we can then learn to understand what is being said through the body by the rest of the world, and the place that is easiest for many to start with is dreaming.

Our modern understanding is that dreaming is an unconscious process; if this is true, and if the unconscious is also the body, dreaming is therefore a bodily process. One way of looking at what is happening with dreaming is that it is the body attempting to translate experiences into consciousness, rather than consciousness translating experiences of the body.

Of course not everything in dream has profound importance, but often times our dreams do hold mysteries which deal with the world to which we do not normally direct our attention. For instance, we may dream of a tooth falling out, which many see as the body conveying the need for something to leave our life that is no longer necessary. Or we may dream of being in a vehicle which we cannot stop, which often is interpreted as a bodily sense of loss of control.

Here we might ask, "where are such messages actually coming from?" The answer to this is complicated, but on the most basic level, they are coming from the body itself. However, since the body is always in relation to the world around it, whether we sleep or are awake, no message can be truly said to be "only" from the body. Instead, every such message is the body's response, just as pain is a response to something.

Consider: when we touch a tree, we experience the tree through the body. We only "feel" the tree because there is a tree there that we are touching. Without the body touching the tree, there is no message of a tree being touched.

So when we dream, our body is conveying a message just as pain is a message. And just as pain can be a message relayed by the body from an external or internal cause, dreams can likewise be from internal or external causes, with the body being the messenger.

Recall again the matter of sleep and the dead which Kadmus mentioned in his book, *True to the Earth*:

This idea of sleep touching death is also well attested to in the ancient world, and it is not original to Heraclitus. It was (and still is in many cultures) a common truth that the dead speak to us in our sleep. More potently, there is a longstanding tradition in both Greek and Roman culture that dreams come through two gates, a gate of truth and one of falsehood, and both gates are found in the Underworld land of the dead. In fact, sleep and dream are often identified with the gates to the Underworld. [64]

We are "unconscious" during sleep, meaning that we are fully experiencing the world only through the body, without the focused attention of conscious mind. Thus, we are more open to hearing outside ourselves, though of course we do not always know how to translate what we hear.

One dream I had recently was of my grandfather telling me I was dying. When I woke, I learned that there had been a fire in the house while I slept that could have killed me. Dreams of dead relatives are rare for me, and so when I wake I try to give what they said particular attention.

Other such dreams that have had profound meaning for me have been dreams of certain animals, or people I did not know telling me strange things which made no sense to me immediately but later unfolded into deep wisdom.

Starting from such dream experiences, I then learned to let unconscious body communicate things to me during waking, as well. It was in this way I began to understand that the feelings I had in certain physical places were not just random,

64. Kadmus. (2018). *True To The Earth*. Gods&Radicals Press

but rather bodily responses to something in the place itself. Near specific trees, for instance, or specific streams, certain feelings came over me that I learned indicated a presence in the place.

Again, though, this sort of knowledge of spirits is only possible once you've learned to discern what the body is communicating. You may feel really good in a place because you just drank some coffee or are with friends, or really sad in a place because you are tired. Or, on the other hand, those feelings may be the body experiencing an Other.

You can only know the difference when you first know the body.

THE FIRES OF MEANING

In each of the previous chapters, I've attempted to describe the Pagan framework through a largely objective narrative. That is, rather than stating too explicitly my own beliefs or describing many of my own practices, I've written more broadly and avoided anything that might seem a bit bizarre.

However, we're now at the point where I cannot write about being Pagan without writing about my own experience and what that has looked like, regardless of how "crazy" that may sound.

So, I'll start with a statement: "Óðinn told me to join a gym."

Perhaps that sounds absurd, so I can rewrite that sentence in a way that sounds a bit less "crazy," such as: "it was because of Óðinn that I joined a gym."

Unfortunately, that rewritten statement isn't actually true. It was actually because of me that I joined a gym. That was my choice, my decision. Óðinn didn't make me get a gym membership, and I didn't get a gym membership because I was trying to make Óðinn happy, and as far as I know, it wasn't even Óðinn's idea, but rather mine.

So, the only way to say this is, "Óðinn told me to join a gym."

To tell you this, though, is to obscure an entire story for which that statement is mere shorthand. So, I will start again, without concern for how crazy or bizarre it might all sound.

"IF THEY WERE ACTUALLY REAL..."

This story actually starts a little over nine years ago with a really haphazard and irresponsible action I don't recommend anyone take. I remember the day well, and precisely where I was standing and what I had been doing before. It was late afternoon, and I was walking home from work and talking aloud to myself.

I've always done that. I think to be a writer you must do this, no matter how embarrassing it can be if someone overhears you. I speak ideas aloud, form sentences before I have written them, and often say "oh" or "hmm" or even "ah! I get it now..." when thinking about some idea or another.

That day, though, standing on a particular part of the sidewalk, about to turn down an alley down which my house was found, I said something quite strange.

"You know, it's too bad gods aren't actually real. Because if they were actually real, it would be a lot of fun to do things for them."

Anyone reading this with experience of gods is no doubt cringing at what I'd done. I cringe sometimes too, and also laugh a bit, and sometimes shake my head whenever I think on that.

What happened next was probably inevitable. I say "next," but what I really mean is "starting from that point on through the next nine years up until now and probably for the rest of my life."

Of course, nothing happened immediately. It isn't as if some bolt of lightning crashed directly in front of me, or a god appeared, or anything like that. It was all a bit gradual, really, and subtle, and also quite sneaky of them.

I started having dreams. Strange ones, with imagery quite jumbled but otherwise more vivid than those to which I'd been earlier accustomed. Sometimes what happened in those dreams—which really never made much sense immediately—lingered in mind all day in the way that an after-image of a bright light stays on your retina even after you close your eyes.

They started slow, quite subtly. I would wake with a sense I had been somewhere else all night, like I had not really been in my bed. Sometimes I felt deeply tired after such dreams; other times, oddly rested.

I told no one, and tried to ignore the dreams. However, the more I tried to ignore them, the more persistent they tended to be. And that's when the dreams stopped waiting for me to be asleep to start.

I remember the first time that happened. I had just gotten into bed with my partner already asleep next to me. The moment I closed my eyes, well before I'd actually fallen asleep, I saw a woman's face staring at me.

So I opened my eyes. I'd seen that face before in my dreams, and though it was a friendly face the dreams with that woman were always really exhausting and I didn't want to dream about her that night. I wanted just to sleep, so I kept my eyes open a little longer, staring into the darkness of the bedroom, and then finally closed them again.

She was there again, so I opened my eyes. I remember saying something to her, maybe aloud but probably just silently. "Hey, can you wait please? I just want to sleep."

I heard no response, but she also wasn't there the next time I closed my eyes. I felt relieved, and then fell into sleep and into another dream with her there.

"...AND WHAT'S IN-BETWEEN THE RAIN"

I have a name for her, by the way. I'm pretty sure it is her name: Brighid. I'm sure it's her name, actually, because a man in a different dream told me that was her name. "It's Brighid," he said. "You can tell by the way the rain falls, and what's in-between the rain."

She was usually laughing about something in those dreams, and throwing wood on a fire. She never spoke to me, or not directly. Sometimes in the dream I didn't feel like she even actually noticed I was there, but that's not precisely correct. It was more that my being there didn't matter much, in the same way that we might notice a spider in the corner of a room but not feel any need to say hello to it.

I eventually made peace with these dreams, stopped fighting them and just let them happen. They got easier once I did this, though no less intense.

Also, when I stopped trying to keep them away, I began to have other kinds of dreams, or dreams with other kinds of images and people. A few of the other people had names, too, and turned out to be gods. Many of them remained unnamed in my dreams, and sometimes I dreamed of gods but there was nobody resembling a person at all.

In fact, this latter sort of dream became the most common. I suspect that's because faces aren't really something the gods have, or not like what we think of as faces. I don't know pre-cisely what they have, just that they sometimes have faces in dreams.

Or maybe they have faces when we need them to. The Greeks and Romans thought of them as having faces, enough to give them faces on statues they made of them. However, the faces on those statues are never the same face, and it's not really the faces that distinguish them.

Similar to the way the Catholic church depicts saints, what is most important in the Greek and Roman statues—as well as Hindu images of gods—is something they are holding, rid-ing, or wearing. Just as you know it's Saint Catherine because the statue is holding a wheel, you know it is Minerva because there is an owl on her shoulder, Ganesha because he is riding a mouse, or Neptune because he's holding a trident.

The gods in my dreams didn't have such easy keys, though when Brighid was around in one of them there was either a soft, barely perceptible rain or a hearth fire nearby. In dreams, there was a tower or stars when it was Arianrhod, and always a cauldron or a skull when it was Ceridwen.

BEING SOMEWHERE ELSE

The problem is that they didn't just stay in my dreams. I say "problem," and that sounds kind of rude perhaps, but it's the correct word to use, because when you are standing in a bar or at a bus stop or in the middle of having sex and you feel the same weird feelings that you feel when they're there in your dreams, it can be a bit disruptive.

Most of that, by the way, was Dionysus. That's the name I have for him, though he never specifically told me it was him. This name I figured out because I met someone else, a human, who told me his experiences of Dionysus were similar to what I was experiencing in those moments.

Dionysus became a kind of initiator for all this, or better said a guide. When I had really intense experiences, visions, and dreams that made no sense to me, it was usually Dionysus who was around to help them make sense.

What did that look like? Oh, this is not easy to describe. First, the experiences themselves were quite bizarre, including having flashes of knowledge about something that was just about to happen, or something that had just happened to someone else. Sometimes I would hear a conversation between between people I didn't recognise, "hear" as if with my ears though no one else around me seemed to have heard it (though I didn't ask—I didn't want anyone to think I was crazy).

Some of these experiences were quite physical. I'd feel someone touch me but there was no one apparently there. Quite often I would feel someone breathing on my neck (that's Brân, I now know). Sometimes it was just the way the wind fell on my skin, but there was no wind.

Other times, these experiences fit into what moderns might call "the supernatural," but which a Pagan framework still insists are fully natural, albeit unusual. One time I was walking to work and suddenly wasn't "there." Instead, I was on a shoreline that I recognised, a stretch of beach near a village of Bretagne I'd visited a decade before. I looked around, felt the salt wind on my lips and in my nose, heard the sand under my feet. I looked again, and I was on the sidewalk again, still walking to work.

Understandably, it was a bit difficult to focus on work that day, and many other days while all those experiences were happening. I could still perform all my duties, but both my desire to do so and my sense of purpose for it all (I was a social worker at a homeless shelter) had deeply diminished.

Around that time, I met a man who became a close friend. Our meeting had been quite by chance: it was at a bar, and I heard someone tell me to go talk to him. There was "no one" there, of course, or not a human, anyway. It was the same voice I heard some other times, and I learned quickly that taking the suggestions it offered always led to profound, life-changing events.

The friendship that arose from that "chance meeting" became deeply transformative, leading me later to other experiences and understandings which eventually brought me to where I am now, writing this book.

"MERE CO-INCIDENCE"

To try to apply a modern, rational analysis to all these events is certainly possible. One might suggest I had a schizophrenic break perhaps, or some process of trauma which my mind healed from by conjuring useful fantasies. And for other events which I'm about to narrate, the response would be "mere co-incidence," which is our modern answer for anything we cannot easily explain.

During the same time as all these other events occurred, I'd briefly met a person to whom I'd recounted some of these events. While he considered himself an atheist, he had shrugged and said it all sounded reasonable regardless. We exchanged contact information, though he was moving to Ireland for work a few weeks later.

We didn't actually keep in contact, though, which is how such things go. I'd heard nothing from him at all for almost a year, until I received an odd email from him. He'd told me he'd "seen" me in Dublin multiple times one day, turning a corner or walking into a store. He'd thought it strange and a bit amusing, and the next day, while visiting the Brú na Bóinne neolithic site (better known as Newgrange), he'd done something he confessed he thought was silly.

"I put your name in for their solstice lottery. I don't think you should get excited, they get 40,000 or so entries every year so the chances are nil. Still, I thought you should know."

The purpose of this lottery is to select 50 people to have a chance to witness a rare and profound event. During the mid-winter solstice, just at sunrise, assuming the morning is clear, a shaft of light shines into the 6000 year old passage tomb for a few short minutes. The tomb is very small: only a small number of people can be safely inside, and there is never any guarantee it will be clear those winter mornings.

Still, when I read his email, I had a feeling of panic. "That will happen," I said aloud, as if I'd already seen it happen.

Three months later, I received this email:

> Dear Rhyd,
>
> I am writing to you from Brú na Bóinne Visitor Centre to let you know that your application form to attend the Winter Solstice at Newgrange, Co Meath, Ireland was one of those picked out by local school children on September 26th 2014. There were 30,532 applications altogether. Many congratulations!

They selected 50 out of that total number, putting the probability of *not* being selected at 99.84%. My chances of being selected, then, were *16 out of 10,000.* Of course, that isn't a zero percent chance, and the chances of being selected for that are much better than winning most financial lotteries.

That being said, I don't know how to calculate the chances of a person you only ever met once and had no real communication with after that thinking he saw you multiple times in a foreign city and then deciding to put your name in to a cultural lottery, rather than his own.

The Newgrange passage tomb, in Irish lore, is said to be the home of The Dagda, a god who said to be the father of Brighid. That is of course also possible to put down to "mere co-incidence," but regardless it meant something to me. Other "chance" meetings happened there, and during the rest of my trip. I traveled to Wales while there, hiked around to the site where two dragons were said to be buried under a hill.

Beyond some really intense dreams full of people telling me things I "needed to know" during that part of my trip, I had an experience there I cannot really describe, though I have tried many times to do so. Standing on the hill overlooking a Welsh lake[65] in a midwinter rain, I saw something through a rain drop dripping from a tree that made everything else in my life make sense.

I don't know what to call what I saw, but I sometimes call it "dragon fire." It wasn't fire, and there was no dragon, but it was something "dragon fire" nevertheless accurately de-scribes. It was something from the earth, from within the earth, but something also within myself.

Another word for it might be "will." It was something older than machines, as old as forests, maybe even older. Something both within and without, something connecting me—my body, my history, and everything I was—to everything else around me.

65. The specific place was the hill of Dinas Emrys overlooking Llyn Dinas in the province of Gwynedd, Wales. This was the site of the two buried dragons mentioned in the chapter "Gods and Spirits."

It was that moment I understood something I had tried to understand for a long time. I didn't need to believe the right things, or believe in gods, or believe in magic. I just needed *to be*, to let those things be, and be with all of that without trying to make sense of anything anymore.

By being, I became. By being, what happened around me and what I did acted in concert, like it was all some orchestrated symphony or dance which everyone—human and non-human—has known from even before their births.

WAS WILLST DU?

That event led to many others in my life, eventually leading me to encountering more gods and land spirits, including a certain figure I've encountered twice "in person."

The first time I met him, he was just a strange guy giving me a bizarre look from one eye as he walked past me on a path near an old druidic site in Bretagne. Later that night, I saw him again in dream, and he made me an offer I politely inclined.

The next time, however, we actually spoke in person. It was my last day on a long pilgrimage through Europe, which I had ended by staying with a friend in Berlin. On that final day, just before catching a train to the airport from which I would then return to the United States, I decided to buy an ice cream cone and sit on a park bench one last time.

I had an hour before I needed to leave, and I just wanted some time alone to think, to enjoy the fleeting minutes of my experience in Europe. I was profoundly sad: I didn't want to leave, and I felt like my entire life made more sense when I was there than it ever did in America.

I was interrupted. A man had walked by, dressed in torn clothing, with long grey scraggly hair, and he then decided to sit directly next to me on that bench, rather than on either of the two adjacent empty benches.

I'll admit to being frustrated. He was sitting uncomfortably close. I worked professionally with homeless people for six years, and he looked homeless, and this all reminded me of the job I didn't want to return to in the country in which I no longer wanted to live.

I looked up and asked him if he wanted money or a cigarette.

"No," he answered.

"Then what do you want?" I asked, probably quite rudely.

"*Nein*," he said in German. "*Was willst du?*"[66]

That's when I noticed his glass eye.

I shrugged. "I want to live in Europe."

He nodded. "Okay," he replied, then said some other things I still don't fully understand. Then, he stood up and left.

I heard him again a few years later, though in a backwards way, the way you hear with your body instead of just your

---

66 "No, what do **you** want?"

ears. I was living in Europe, as I said I had wanted to. And I was not in a good situation, and was feeling quite a bit of despair. I felt disconnected from myself, from the world around me, and frozen in place.

He told me I should join a gym, because I obviously wanted to and so I should do what I truly desired. So I did, and found that this was what I had been missing, a direct way to be body again rather than becoming stuck "in my head."

That's what I mean when I said, "Óðinn told me to join a gym," a statement which makes no sense without the rest of that context.

Context is also why I've saved all this for the very end. Life is an enchanted thing, the body is capable of understanding things we rarely allow ourselves to experience, nature has a rhythm and song of its own, our ancestors understood things we desperately need to remember, the land speaks, and gods and spirits dwell everywhere. All this that I have written about I have learned because of these experiences, from letting myself be body and giving attention to the time of the moon, the seasons, and the stars rather than the logic of machines.

This is what it has looked like for me. For you, it may look different. I don't suggest the specific stumbling and clumsy path I took to get here, nor do I recommend loudly stating that you think it would be fun to do things for gods "if they really existed."

You can live a deeply enchanted life without doing all that, and likely a more stable life than I've necessarily had. Since that very first experience, I've lived in quite a few cities in quite a few countries, lived in no shortage of bizarre situations and experienced no small amount of weird visions, dreams, and other moments that still don't make much sense to me.

It is enough to go for a walk and to stare at the moon. It is enough to think fondly on your ancestors, to light an occasional candle in their memory, to leave an offering to a house spirit once in a while. It is also enough just to let yourself feel the sun on your skin, to enjoy the feel of water or the touch of grass under your bare feet.

It is enough just to be, without worrying about believing the right things or seeking experiences outside of what we have come to expect as usual. Being Pagan is itself enough, because it is most of all being yourself, recollecting the lost parts of you and remembering them in a way that feels more human and less machine.

All this is an act of joy, of life, and of nature itself, which is what being Pagan really is.

PAGAN RITUALS

Throughout this book, I've made reference to many acts which help towards being Pagan. In many other books, it's common to write these out as "exercises" as if you are reading a self-help book or a collection of recipes. This book is neither of those, and anyway the point to all this is to help you reclaim a sense of agency and active relation to the world, rather than just doing what someone else tells you to do.

With that said, however, I know some readers would benefit from more concrete rituals, so I've included some here. These are all things I have done, and they do not derive from ancient occult grimoires nor from divine revelation, only from my own experience.

LOOK AT THE MOON

This is where everything begins, and it is the simplest ritual possible. Look for and at the moon every day, even the slightest glimpse. Don't use external guides to find it, but rather just look for it yourself. You won't find it everyday, nor will you find it at the same time each day, but look anyway.

After months (many moons) of doing so, you will begin to already know where and when it will be, and what face it will have. Keep looking, and let the time of the moon become its own rhythm in your life.

MARK THE SEASONS

The rhythm of the earth's seasons is a yearly cycle that affects all of living nature, including humans. Rivers swell and diminish according to the seasons, plants grow and die back, animals mate, give birth, and hide away, and we humans unconsciously (bodily) respond to these shifts as well.

A very simple ritual to align your conscious attention to the unconscious reality of the seasons is to mark each shift with a small celebration. Depending on where you live, the official calendar dates of these shifts (mid-June, mid-September, mid-December, and mid-March) or older Celtic and Germanic dates (the first of February, the first of May, the first of August, and the first of November) might fit best as days to celebrate.

Regardless of which you choose, create a way to celebrate, such as hosting a small dinner, visiting important places to you, or participating in local celebrations.

GO FOR A WALK

Besides looking at the moon, the most basic and also most important act you can do that will bring you into closer relation to the world around you is going for a meandering, purposeless walk in the place you live.

The key here is to stroll, to wander, to move about the world with a kind of openness that moderns usually avoid. Often we close ourselves off to the world around us, stare at our phones and listen to music rather than letting the world around us in.

So, do the opposite. Leave your phone at home and just walk. Let yourself hear the sounds, smell the scents the world gives off, feel the wind, sun, and rain on your skin, taste the air around you, and regard the land with eyes open.

BE BODY AGAIN

This is deeply related to the previous ritual, since walking is a way to align your consciousness back into the body you are. There are other ways to do this as well, each with its own knowledge.

When you observe a child, you will notice that he or she seems to experience a relentless joy just being. Playing, jumping, running, crawling, and all the other physical acts of a child's existence seem to be acts of pure delight. The taste of foods they enjoy, the feel of grass under their bare feet, the tickle of the wind, the warmth of sunlight on skin, and many other "simple" pleasures seem to be causes for grand celebration and laughter.

Do this, too. Go walk barefoot in the grass. Nap in a warm sun, catch snowflakes on your tongue. Play-wrestle with a friend, eat a meal with fragrant herbs, go swimming or take a very long bath. These are all things moderns call "self-care," but they are ultimately the core acts of being body.

If you are able and it interests you, join a gym, learn yoga, or sign up for a martial arts class or sports club. Or go running if you can, even just very short distances. Do strenuous things that help you feel the body you are, activities that gently push the limits of what you thought you were capable of.

CARETAKING OUR KIN

It is not available to all, of course, but two powerful rituals you can add to your life are gardening and caring for animals. When you garden, you learn more about the way the earth and plants work than any book can teach you, and caring for animals is the same.

For those who cannot have animals in their home or have no space for even the smallest garden, there is no reason to despair. The land around you is full of plants and animals, wild flowers and edible "weeds" growing in the cracks of pavement and birds flitting constantly from branch to branch. Consider feeding crows or ravens (whole, unroasted and unsalted peanuts are ideal), or setting up a bird feeder. Gather wildflower seeds and spread them in abandoned lots in early spring. Learn the names of everything that grows and breathes where you live, and tell them your name, too.

ANCESTRAL SHRINES

Every animist, Pagan, and indigenous culture has some form of ancestral veneration, and these continue even into Christianity and civic rituals (such as national holidays for veterans or leaders). Shrines, in particular, are a very widespread practice.

We often create these unconsciously in our own homes, hanging photos of deceased family members in certain places or placing items that remind us of them together in one location. If you find you already have such a place, use that location. If not, create a small space for it and add photos or memorabilia, or just place a very small bowl of water or a tealight (or both) there.

Regularly (daily, weekly, once a moon, once a season, or on specific birthdays) light a candle in that place, or fill the bowl of water, or do some other ritual act and speak a brief prayer of thanks to those who gave you life. If you do not know their names, just call them "ancestors" or "grandparents." I myself do this twice daily, just a few words that takes no more than a few seconds to speak.

HOUSEHOLD SHRINE

Another widespread Pagan practice is the creation of a shrine to household spirits. Such spirits generally do not like "too much" attention, meaning that they do not demand or even like acts of reverence or worship. I find the best way to understand this relationship is that they are a bit like highly-independent cats, who often seem to merely share a home with their humans and want food put out for them, but they don't want your attention unless they are seeking it out first.

Shrines to household spirits are often created either at entrances or in the centre of a house, which traditionally was the hearth (or kitchen). To find an appropriate place in your own home, try to think about one spot where you for some reason never look, a place where dust tends to gather and you rarely place things there, an "invisible" place. My suspicion is that these places are where such spirits already live.

Find such a place, or alternatively choose a corner of a kitchen, an entranceway, or a part of a room that no one will disturb. Light a tealight there sometimes, or leave flower petals, or anything subtle that reminds you and the house spirit know that you appreciate their presence.

SHRINES TO OTHER SPIRITS AND TO GODS

By now you probably understand the basic way a shrine is created. It is a sacred (set-apart) place created to honour something or someone, and they all share this general trait. What differs is the kinds of spaces used, as well as the materials, and how "honouring" manifests in each case.

Something that can be incredibly helpful to do if you are interested in creating shrines is to look to the shrines which already exist where you are. Civic monuments are a kind of shrine, for instance, including memorial plaques. Catholic churches are full of shrines to saints (who are often barely-concealed Pagan gods dressed up in Christian garb), and other religions such as Hinduism and Shinto create all kinds of shrines to gods, spirits, and ancestors. Looking to these other shrines can help you understand how they are created.

The concept of hospitality is also a key feature of these shrines. They are places created for a spirit or a god to feel at home in, a bit like preparing a table for a guest. Other aspects of hospitality are helpful to remember, such as what kinds of things a guest prefers. Thus, a shrine to a land spirit is best created from aspects of the land itself, rather than industrially-produced materials or statues. A shrine to a god would contain items associated with that god (a shrine to Thor would might have oak leaves or bark, for example, or be carved of oak).

Candles and incense are both very common things to include and use in such shrines, though be mindful of not burning candles in places where melted paraffin wax (which is an industrial product) would pollute nature. Also, avoid leaving "offerings" that would in other circumstances be seen as trash (especially plastic and metal).

Alternatively, you can create one shrine in your home where you honour spirits and gods, speaking prayers to them while you light a candle. Such prayers need not be formal—mine definitely are not.

UNDERSTANDING ENCHANTMENT

One of the most powerful rituals I think a person can do that will help them sense the way that our consciousness and unconsciousness work together is one recommended by the writer Marie Kondo (also known as Konmari). In her "Konmari method," she teaches people to organize their lives by holding possessions in their hands, asking themselves if the item "sparks joy," and then if not, thanking the item for its existence and finding a respectful way to part with the object.

This method is ultimately animist, derived from Shinto understandings of the *kami* and our relationship to them. Often, we develop relations to certain objects or places that we are not conscious of because we did so bodily; because we rarely prioritise our bodily relationship to the world, we do not always understand the implications of these relationships.

Taking the basic principle of the "Konmari method," which is at its core an animist principle, you can develop rituals to transform your relationships to places and objects. Perhaps there are spots in your home where you do not feel comfortable, or places in your neighbourhood that always provoke certain feelings of despair, depression, anxiety, or fear. On the other hand, you probably have articles of clothing you wear when you want to feel good, or places you visit that always give you a sense of happiness or hope.

With a spirit of curiosity, go to such places or hold such objects and ask questions aloud. Speak to the place or the thing, voice how you feel, and listen for a bodily sense of what is occurring or has occurred between you and the place or object.

Again, it is vital to keep in a state of curiosity, rather than one of certainty. Being body is a way of being that many of us need years and years to re-learn, and often times our initial conclusion about a matter is shaped more by society or mass media than by our true bodily experience.

A PLAGUE OF GODS

CULTURAL APPROPRIATION AND THE RESURGENT LEFT SACRED

A little over six years ago now, I received a demand which asked me to use my influence and my publishing platform to help denounce someone. I read the demand with curiosity and a bit of worry. The message stated in rather vague language that the sender had been asked by "the indigenous community" to help stamp out all acts of appropriation of their cultural and religious forms by white people. And the best way to do this, according to him, was to put mass social pressure on a particular white woman who was about to host a workshop.

My reply was ambiguous and non-committal. "Thanks. I'll look into this," I wrote back, and then did exactly that.

The message bothered me a bit, especially due to the strange claims by the author. There is no such thing as "the indigenous community," for instance, but rather countless indigenous communities. Nor did I know of any such communities investing specific white people to be the defender of their sacred cultural practices.

What bothered me most, however, was that the woman to be denounced was not actually claiming to make or to teach people an indigenous rite or practice. I asked the activist about this, and his hostile reply gave me my first taste of what the arguments around cultural appropriation would soon become.

"White people should stick to their own practices instead of appropriating other people's spirituality."

This statement startled me, as I was in the midst of researching several neopagan groups aligned with far-right and white nationalist ideas. For these groups—whose beliefs were based around exclusion, genetic ancestry, and separatism—white people should only worship "European" gods, and such gods shouldn't be worshiped by others. That is, gods like Thor or Lugh were only for "white" people and for no one else.

In the end, I declined to help denounce the woman, and instead watched in shock at the streams of abusive behaviour towards her by quite a few people who'd answered this call instead. Remarkably few of those people self-identified as indigenous—many of them were also "white"—but no one else seemed to notice this. They succeeded: the workshop was canceled, and a victory was declared over cultural appropriation.

That event particularly haunts me, especially since I have seen it repeated in countless other iterations: social media crusades, pressure campaigns, and boycotts against individuals deemed "appropriative" of indigenous, or African, or Asian, or any other spiritual or cultural forms. In some cases these crusades are understandable; for instance against shops selling Native American ceremonial head dresses, or individuals claiming to teach Haitian Voodoo with no relationship to Haitian practitioners, or "Enlightenment Centers" dispensing *ayahuasca* or other entheogenic substances to urban professionals looking for ways to become more in touch with themselves.

In many more instances, however, the targets haven't been people trying to make money off of religious or cultural forms. Instead, they were people adopting forms and practices that "belong to others." Such forms and practices include, among many others: wearing certain hair styles, make-up, or jewellery (dreadlocks, henna, mohawks, hoop earrings, bangles, winged eyeliner); eating certain foods (collard greens, fry bread) or even entire cuisines (such as Mexican, Chinese, or Indian); using certain words or manners of speech (including words "belonging" to gay or black people); and especially spiritual practices (including Tarot, Yoga, and entire religious traditions like Buddhism, Hinduism, Sufism, and Kabbala). And while in many cases the target is someone identified as a white person, there are also many examples of black people accused of appropriating indigenous cultural forms, or people of Asian descent accused of stealing or appropriating from black communities.

These many debates, accusations, and excesses around cultural appropriation can all get quite messy, understandably leading many to completely abandon even trying to avoid it. On the other side, there are some who deny these obvious excesses occur, or entrench in grand political narratives which paint groups of people (often but not always white people) as "inherently appropriative."

For those who truly wish not to do harm, to not oppress or steal from others, and also for those who truly wish to support and protect the recovery, growth, and continuation of the ancestral and cultural forms of oppressed peoples, cultural appropriation is a deeply important concept. Causing unnecessary harm and offence to people, especially to those who have suffered political subjugation by Empire, is something many people understandably wish to avoid. Unfortunately, the concept of cultural appropriation and the current arguments against it have drifted into a strange and unnavigable space wherein any adoption of another culture's forms, style of dress, language, and food can be seen as appropriative, harmful, and oppressive.

This current understanding presents several problems and can lead to something even more dangerous than the harm it attempts to prevent. First of all, the concept is no longer rooted (if it ever previously was) in a historical understanding of how cultures are formed, how they change, and how they are delineated. This leads to the second problem, which is that arguments about who should and who should not be allowed to wear, eat, believe, worship, or practice things enforce notions of cultural, racial, and ethnic separatism that mirror nationalist and monotheist fears regarding miscegenation,[67] cultural mixing, and foreign pollution. Third, despite attempting to fight imperialist colonial forms of oppression, the concept now reproduces a uniquely Western capitalist framework in which even sacred cultural forms—just like air, water, and other parts of the world previously exempt from economic logic—are subject to the logic of privatization and commodification.

THE DRIFTED MEANING OF CULTURAL APPROPRIATION

How a concept meant to protect indigenous cultural forms from exploitation became instead an argument for racial separatism and a reproduction of capitalist property relations is unclear. Often times in discussions[68] the concept is presented and debated without reference to its theoretical framework, which can cause drift in the meaning of a concept, especially when there is no agreement nor mediator on what the concept actually means. For instance, consider how concepts like "toxic masculinity" or "BIPOC" often have two

67. Intermarriage between people of different "races."

68. Especially via social media like Tumblr, and Twitter, where anonymity is easy and claimed authority is impossible to verify.

completely different meanings operating in the same arguments. Toxic masculinity, for instance, can mean "masculinity that is toxic" to some while also meaning "masculinity is inherently toxic" to others. BIPOC has two meanings now: "people of color who are Black or Indigenous" (*excluding* other people of color, for instance Chinese or other Asian immigrants) and also "Black, Indigenous, and other people of color" (*including* all people of color, with a special emphasis on Black and Indigenous people). In both instances, the difference in understood meaning is profound.

Cultural appropriation is subject to a similar double-meaning, except in its case the meaning is triple. First of all, the term itself came into use to refer to something completely different than either of the two meanings of the phrase now. As Shuja Haidar explains:

> "...the Left has not always understood "cultural appropriation" as a form of oppression. This connotation of the term has become ubiquitous in today's social media-driven political climate. But when it first came into use, "cultural appropriation" denoted very nearly the opposite of its contemporary meaning.

> The idea preceded the term, as a product of the Center for Contemporary Cultural Studies at the University of Birmingham. For thinkers like Stuart Hall, cultural appropriation described the way subcultures were created. The contemporary objects of inquiry, in studies like 1975's Resistance Through Rituals, were youth cultures in England: teddy boys, mods, skinheads and so on.

> But the precedents ran deeper. Indian food in England, Negro spirituals in America, bathhouses in 19th-century France — these were all contexts in which members of what

we might now call "marginalized groups" used elements of a dominant culture in altered forms, generating their own communities that could hide in plain sight.[69]

That is, cultural appropriation originally referred to acts by marginalized people to retool dominant cultural forms as their own. As Haidar mentions, the Negro spiritual is a great example of this. In perhaps the most famous spiritual, "Go Down Moses," slaves from Africa appropriated the Jewish story of escape from slavery in Egypt, and were thus able to sing openly about their desire for freedom by using the sacred texts of their Christian masters.

So that is the first meaning of cultural appropriation, one that has at least a neutral (and even positive) connotation. Of course that is not what most people mean by the term now. It now refers to the adoption or theft of marginalized cultural forms by dominant cultures, rather than the adaptation of dominant cultural forms by people in marginalized cultures: *literally the opposite of its original meaning.*

There is a third meaning, however, which is more a literal understanding of the term rather than either of its connotations. But before we look at that one, we need to take an important detour into etymology (the study of the root meanings of words) to see something larger here.

69. Haider, S. (2017, January). "Safety Pins and Swastikas." The Jacobin. https://www.jacobinmag.com/2017/01/safety-pin-box-richard-spencer-neo-nazis-alt-right-identity-politics

THE PROPER AND APPROPRIATE MEANING OF "APPROPRIATION"

While we generally think of appropriation as a kind of theft, appropriation literally means something else: *to set aside or claim as belonging to something or someone.* Its two primary meanings are "to turn into property" and "to set aside" (consider the phrase "budget appropriations," which are funds set aside for a purpose).

These meanings come from its shared Latin root (via French) with the following words:

- proper/improper

- proprietary

- propriety

- appropriate/inappropriate (adj.)

- expropriate

- property

The root word entered English through French as a conflation of two closely related words: *proprete* (from Latin *proprietas,* "special character or quality") and *propre* (from Latin *proprius,* "specific to itself, one's own"). The English meanings of all the related words thus bear the meanings of that combined root, which are:

- intrinsic, innate, or natural quality (as in "healing properties")

- individual, unique ("proper noun," a noun the refers to a unique thing or person)

- apt, fitting ("proper or appropriate attire")

- belonging to or of oneself ("proprietary" and "property," also in the French reflexive use of *propre*: "its own")

- correct ("proper speech")

- clean, set right ("everything in its proper place," seen especially in the non-reflexive French *propre*: "clean")

- distinct, set apart, limited ("the city proper")

Particularly important in all these meanings is that property as we understand it now (something owned or ownable) is a much later meaning of the word that only came into common use during the birth of capitalism in the 17th century. The earlier sense of property as something inherent or intrinsic to a thing morphed into this dominant meaning through the idea that external things (like land) could be seen as a unique, set apart, and intrinsic quality (as in "healing properties") of an individual or group.

Appropriation preserves all these root meanings. To appropriate is to:

- turn something into one's own

- to turn into something that can be or is part of one's self (property)

- to limit a thing as reserved for an individual or a group

- to set a thing apart from other things

In all these meanings it parallels the English legal concept of "Enclosure," the parceling of common land into separate plots for sale and ownership.

So, cultural appropriation literally denotes a kind of parceling out or dividing of culture for ownership, taking its qualities and nature for one's own and excluding others from it. Of course, that's not how it's actually used now. Instead, cultural appropriation generally means, as recorded by the *Oxford English Dictionary*,

> the unacknowledged or inappropriate adoption of the customs, practices, ideas, etc. of one people or society by members of another and typically more dominant people or society.

Note the re-appearance in that definition of appropriate as the adjectival "inappropriate," which brings us one other core meaning of proper/property/propriety/appropriate: that of "rightness" or "correctness." This is again inherited from the French word *propre*, whose non-reflexive meaning is "clean" (*les vaisselles sont propres*/the dishes are clean). Another way of translating this meaning is "back to their nature" (that is, undirtied, uncontaminated—basically: "pure").

So, in this definition, cultural appropriation is inappropriate because it puts cultural forms where they should not be. It is not proper (clean, true, correct) to adopt someone else's culture, because those things should be kept separate (just as property is separate, unique, set apart, exclusive).

THE ENCLOSED CULTURAL COMMONS

So we find really two contradictory logics within the concept of cultural appropriation. The first is its literal definition: *the turning of culture into property or adopting cultural forms as one's own, or the enclosing of cultural forms for private rather than public use.* However, the common understanding of the concept means the opposite: *the theft of cultural property owned by or inherit/intrinsic to specific peoples or groups.*

Let's look now at the way arguments about cultural appropriation often occur, especially in the United States. Though the political theories employed in these arguments vary, they are all based upon a belief in cultural "property," that there are practices, clothing and hair styles, foods, and beliefs that can be—and are—owned or intrinsic to one people and should not be used or adopted by others. That is, cultural forms are private property, and only the owners of those cultural forms may participate in, practice, or use them.

Who precisely has the authority to makes decisions about the use of that property is not always clear, since cultural forms (unlike books or songs, for example) cannot easily be traced to an author or authority, only a cultural, racial, or identity group. And of course, no group is monolithic, so the determination on whether a cultural form is being appropriated is usually up to people who appoint themselves representatives for that group.

This can be seen best in a recent essay written by an anonymous group of North American people of claimed Romani descent, titled: "Your Tarot Card Practice is Romani Cultural Appropriation."[70] The essay offers no evidence that Tarot cards are a spiritual practice that originated with the Romani; in fact, it is quite defensive of anyone who might ask for such evidence:

> "it's tiresome that we once again need to cater to white people by providing 'sources' that they are either just going to ignore or use to appropriate us anyway"

The essay then admits that there is no agreement among the Romani that non-Romani shouldn't be allowed to read Tarot:

> "Tarot is CLOSED. Yes, there are Romani people who say it's not. But don't you want to err on the side of caution and just be conservative about your practices?... So please get it through your heads, people, many of us ARE NOT OKAY with you using Tarot cards. I don't care if you are white or not. I don't care who you are. I don't care what mental or physical health conditions you have. You're not welcome to my practice. Not in a spell or in a private reflective practice...."[71]

This same problem of authority occurs in many other arguments about cultural appropriation as well. For instance, who

70. Anonymous."Your Tarot Card Practice is Romani Cultural Appropriation." (2021, February 15). SLYSCA Patreon. https://www.patreon.com/posts/your-tarot-card-47577597

71. All-caps are theirs, not mine. If you have been practicing Tarot and now realize you have been "stealing," the writers of the essay also have a suggestion for what to do with your cards: "Make confetti - no really, it removes them from circulation and makes a giant mess that you, or someone you love, will have to clean up later, and that may be penance enough for those who really want to punish themselves."

has the authority to say that Yoga should only be practiced by Asians? Who owns dreadlocks—Black Americans or the other peoples who have also worn dreaded hair, including the Ngapa of India, the Cree, Aztec priests, the Poles, the Ancient Greeks and Minoans, and the Massai?

The matter of dreadlocks in particular underlines another problem in many of the conversations about cultural appropriation, because often times an apparent claim to exclusivity or ownership is *historically inaccurate*. For instance, two ritual forms seen as cultural property to indigenous people in North America—sacred drum making and sweating ceremonies—are actually much more widespread. Likewise, a long list of words "exclusive" to AAVE (African American Vernacular English) that was used to police cultural appropriation in many online forums contains quite a few words developed earlier among other English-speaking peoples (including *ain't, y'all*, and even the word "*cunty*," claimed as exclusive property of AAVE but used much earlier in English Cockney and also Australian slang).

We could get quite lost in a long list of such problems, easily and endlessly poking holes in the arguments about appropriation, but the core questions are more important. Is culture "property?" Can culture be "owned?"

That leads us back to the literal definition of cultural appropriation: the turning of culture and cultural forms into property, enclosing or parceling out culture into things that can be owned, bought, and held privately rather than commonly. In this understanding of the concept, we can see immediately that the property logic of capitalism (remembering that the word *property* itself took on an economic sense only after the birth of capitalism) is the primary conceptual framework in the common (non-literal or "social justice") definition of cultural appropriation.

Consider again the cited essay, which essentially claims that the Romani "own" Tarot. The authors argue that, because they believe the Romani are the authors or creators of Tarot, that Tarot is inherently Romani and has an intrinsic Romani property, they therefore have the right to assert an intellectual property right over its use. It is improper for Tarot to be used by others because such use takes it out of its proper place. People who use it without their permission are therefore violating Romani ownership rights, a point that can be seen particularly in the essay's repeated statements that, if someone wants a Tarot divination, they must pay a Romani person to perform it for them.

Asserting ownership and attempting to privatize something that has become common parallels the capitalist logic of property, especially during the birth of capitalism. The repeated use of the word "closed" in their essay about Tarot echoes the capitalist logic of Enclosure, the privatization of something that had been commonly used. We should here remember especially that feudal lords and then the crown held "legal" ownership of the land upon which the commons existed. By enclosing it, the government was in essence re-asserting the right to exclude people from something the people had come to see as non-exclusive.

While it may seem a bit harsh to compare social justice arguments for cultural exclusion to capitalist enclosure and private property, this cannot be ignored. Much of the discourse —especially from American activists—has inherited (or has been colonized by) the capitalist logic of property. In their framework (unacknowledged or not), cultural forms are property belonging to a specific group of people, and using those forms without express permission is theft or trespassing.

THE PROFANED SACRED

However, though the social justice understanding of the problem of cultural appropriation and a more literal understanding seem to be completely opposed to each other (one asserts property rights on culture, the other insists culture cannot be property), they both agree in one area. Both stand as critiques of the commercialization of cultural forms by capitalist corporations and the seizure of sacred artefacts by museums and other institutions. It's in this shared criticism that a kind of re-orientation might occur.

Consider, for example, the British Museum, which is the largest depository of stolen sacred artefacts in the world. Not just the Parthenon ("Elgin") Marbles (Greek polytheist), but also the Maqdala treasures (including Ethiopian artefacts of early Christians and a sacred lock of hair from an emperor), a statue from Easter Island, the Benin Bronzes (sacred sculptures from Africa), and countless other sacred relics (including bones and other body parts) from indigenous cultures across every continent are all held as property by the British Museum.

Likewise, corporations and entrepreneurs constantly commercialize and market spirituality and cultural forms. The American clothing corporation Urban Outfitters, for example, has repeatedly sold merchandise using Navajo and other North American indigenous people's traditional artwork; perfume and make-up corporation Sephora recently sold a commercial "witch kit," and indigenous and traditional dances, clothing, and many other cultural forms are constantly used as marketing for products ranging from soda to automobiles to banking services.

And of course there are the "plastic shamans," the spiritual retreats, conventions, workshops, and media created and led by people who have repackaged sacred traditions into commercial ventures for the professional managerial classes of every city in the world. It's impossible to ignore these things: the ayahuasca retreats, sweat lodge ceremonies, and shamanic journeying quests to help project managers and corporate executives find new inspiration for their teams and companies, charlatans teaching indigenous practices they conjured from their imaginations, and of course the lucrative "spiritual tourism" industry promising to offer connection to authentic and exotic wisdom.

This is all cultural appropriation in its "truest" form, and regardless of which understanding one has on what appropriation actually means, the reaction to these things is usually visceral disgust and anger.

That shared experience points to something deeper going on than mere "inappropriate" adoption of culture. It isn't just that these are acts which steal or enclose spiritual or cultural forms: a sacred violation seems to be occurring. Or as Marx and Engles wrote in *The Communist Manifesto*, referring to the transformative power of the capitalist class, these commercial acts turn the sacred into the profane.

The roots of both the words sacred and profane are also Latin and likewise come to us through French. *Sacred* means something "set apart," something that is holy, put to a dedicated (usually but not always religious) use. *Profane*, on the other hand, means "outside the temple." To profane something was to displace it, to strip it of its sacred nature, to make it mundane, normal, everyday, or banal.

To put it another way, a sacred thing has meaning outside of the everyday, and a profane thing no longer has that meaning and has instead become everyday.

Returning to the contradictory meanings of cultural appropriation, it's obvious that both agree sacred things should not be commercialized, that commercialization, marketing, and the capitalist logic ultimately profanes (cheapens and banalizes) the sacred. The difference between them can then be restated as a difference in the conception of the sacred itself.

THE LEFT AND RIGHT SACRED

We've been slowly pulling at the tangled threads of the matter of cultural appropriation, and we need to do a little more tugging in order to get to the core problem. To this, we need to make one more apparent diversion, which is not a diversion at all but rather the primary of the knot: the sacred itself.

In many Arabic cultures (which inherited this division from their pre-Islamic animist ancestors), as well as many other cultures, there is a division between the left and right hands according to what they can be used for. One hand (the right hand) is considered clean and therefore can be used for tasks like eating or cooking, and that hand can also be offered to another person (for touch, as in a handshake or to help stabilize someone who is falling). The other hand, the left hand, is considered unclean, not to be offered to others and not to be used for eating. However, the left hand does have its own uses: for instance, it is used in urination or defecation, as well as for cleaning the body afterwards, and also for touching dead bodies or other "impure" things.

It would seem at first glance that the right hand—the clean hand—is a sacred hand, since it is set apart (one of the meanings of sacred) from the dirtying tasks associated with toilet activities. And this is true, but it does not tell the whole story. The left hand, also, has a sacred nature, specifically because it is set apart for touching unclean things and ultimately making sure that the right hand is able maintain its sacred "pure" role.

This division between a left and a right sacred is not limited to hands, nor to Arabic cultures. In fact, similar divisions exist in almost every known culture (including "secular" ones), a kind of "binary" sacred in which the sacred itself is divided between two orientations.

Consider for example the purity codes found in the Torah regarding menses, semen, and genital discharge:

> When a man has an emission of semen, he must bathe his whole body with water, and he will be unclean till evening. Any clothing or leather that has semen on it must be washed with water, and it will be unclean till evening. When a man lies with a woman and there is an emission of semen, both must bathe with water, and they will be unclean till evening.

> When a woman has her regular flow of blood, the impurity of her monthly period will last seven days, and anyone who touches her will be unclean till evening. Anything she lies on during her period will be unclean, and anything she sits on will be unclean. Whoever touches her bed must wash his clothes and bathe with water, and he will be unclean till evening. Whoever touches anything she sits on must wash his clothes and bathe with water, and he will be unclean till evening. Whether it is the bed or anything she was sitting on, when anyone touches it, he will be unclean till evening.

> If a man lies with her and her monthly flow touches him, he will be unclean for seven days; any bed he lies on will be unclean. [72]

72. Various. (1973). *The Bible*, Leviticus 15: 16–24 (NIV ed.). Bible Hub, https://biblehub.com/leviticus/15-16.htm.

While many modern interpretations of these codes (and other prohibitions, for instance those against wearing mixed-fabric clothing or eating certain foods) interpret them as a kind of hygiene, this reading ignores the repeated references to sin, abomination, and the need for atonement required, especially for women:

> When she is cleansed from her discharge, she must count off seven days, and after that she will be ceremonially clean. On the eighth day she must take two doves or two young pigeons and bring them to the priest at the entrance to the Tent of Meeting. The priest is to sacrifice one for a sin offering and the other for a burnt offering. In this way he will make atonement for her before the LORD for the uncleanness of her discharge.
>
> You must keep the Israelites separate from things that make them unclean, so they will not die in their uncleanness for defiling my dwelling place, which is among them.[73]

The "impure" quality of semen and menses in ancient Jewish law—as well as other cultures—probably comes from older animist beliefs about ancestors and spirits entering the body through those fluids, especially since they are both associated ultimately with new life. Rituals and ceremonies were required to deal with these substances because they held the very power of life within them (and were sometimes even seen as places where there was no boundary between this-world and the Otherworld or the divine). So though they were later re-labeled as "impure" and defiling by priests enforcing

---

73. Various. (1973). *The Bible*, Leviticus 15: 28–31 (NIV ed.). Bible Hub, https://biblehub.com/leviticus/15-16.htm.

monotheism onto previously animist Hebrews, the purity rituals and sacrifices continue the belief that semen and menses were sacred.[74]

In addition, the directives on what to do with any objects that touched these sacred substances tell us more about their otherworldly nature. Clay pots that came in contact with them were to be broken so they could never be used, wooden tools needed to be thoroughly cleaned, and everything else that touched these substances (including other people) also needed to undergo cleansing rituals. This all points to an attempt to keep the "impure" sacred from spreading into mundane, everyday life, just as many African animist peoples performed long rituals to make sure the gods and spirits stayed in the otherworld, rather than invading the mundane world.[75]

The left sacred is a transgressive sacred, a sacred that seeks to spread and contaminate the rest of life with its power. The other hand of the sacred, seen in the purity codes of Leviticus, is the right sacred, the sacred that polices the borders between the sacred and the profane with an aim to stop the sacred from spreading to places where it cannot be controlled any longer.

74. For more on this, see Grey, P., & Dimech, A. (2016). *The Red Goddess*. SCARLET IMPRINT | Bibliothèque Rouge.

75. For great discussions about animist cultures and their taboos about menses, semen, other bodily fluids and the dead, and for countless examples of the animist practice of keeping the divine from "spilling out" into the mundane, see Graeber, D., & Sahlins, M. (2017). *On Kings*. HAU.

The concerns of the right sacred are order, separation, and purity, with a particular focus on preventing syncretic practice and intermixing. We can see this concern immediately in the Judaic prohibitions against eating foods containing both milk and meat in the same dish or wearing clothing containing threads from different sources. Much more obvious—and often violent—in these texts are the divine decrees about preventing intermarriage or allowing those animist and polytheist beliefs (and the people who hold them) to survive:

> ...let nothing that breathes remain alive, but you shall utterly destroy them: the Hittite and the Amorite and the Canaanite and the Perizzite and the Hivite and the Jebusite, just as the LORD your God has commanded you, lest they teach you to do according to all their abominations which they have done for their gods, and you sin against the LORD your God.[76]

> ..utterly destroy all the places where the nations which you shall dispossess served their gods, on the high mountains and on the hills and under every green tree. And you shall destroy their altars, break their sacred pillars, and burn their wooden images with fire; you shall cut down the carved images of their gods and destroy their names from that place[77]

Judaic law is hardly the only place such things have occurred, but it is particularly instructive for two primary reasons. First, these laws were recorded during times of political identity formation, a process of struggle between a monothe-

---

76. Various. (1611). *The Bible*, Deuteronomy 20:16–18 (King James Version ed.). Bible Hub, https://biblehub.com/.

77. Various. (1611). *The Bible*, Deuteronomy 12:2–4 (King James Version ed.). Bible Hub, https://biblehub.com/.

istic and authoritarian priest class and a peasant population that resisted this formation.[78] That peasant population constantly "angered" the priests of the one-god by intermixing with neighbouring peoples, adopting "foreign" customs and gods, and constantly returning to their ancestral, animist ways. Thus more and more codes of behaviour were developed, with ever-increasing commands and prohibitions through which the priest class could better define Jewish religious and political identity through hard boundaries between the peasants and their neighbours. These laws show clearly how the right sacred not only tries to keep the sacred in its place and to prevent it from escaping into the everyday life, but also tries to limit the sacred of others, to prevent a foreign sacred from polluting the domestic sacred.

The second reason why these laws are particularly important is because they function as the "ancestral" theological basis of Christianity. Regardless of whether or nor Christianity is actually a continuation of Jewish sacred traditions, because it propagated these texts as part of its own canon of sacred writings (they comprise 77% of the Christian Bible), they became the basis for a global conception of what the sacred is. Not just in the fact that almost a third of the world is Christian, but also that modern Western institutions and cultural forms (including capitalism) were formed from this conceptual inheritance. Our conceptions of the nation-state,

78. I'm deeply indebted to Peter Grey and his book *Lucifer Princeps* for this realization. See Grey, P. (2016). *Lucifer: Princeps*. Scarlet Imprint / Bibliothèque Rouge.

race, identity, colonialism, Democracy, the Enlightenment, and property all stem from the Christian worldview and its Judeo-Christian[79] conception of the sacred.

One wonders what our societies might have looked like had other indigenous frameworks of the sacred formed the foundation of our public and private life, institutions, and communal relations rather than a monotheistic, right sacred. We can glimpse that possibility by noticing what was born from monotheism and the countless people who still suffer from it. The transatlantic slave trade, for example, the colonization of the Americas, the birth of capitalism, the classification of people into race, and especially the great calamity of industrial civilization and climate change were only possible in a framework of a purifying, exclusionary, right sacred, absent its transgressive, syncretic, and boundary-defying left sacred.

PURIFIED TO DEATH

The right sacred commands the destruction of foreign shrines, foreign gods, and foreign practices in order to keep a people pure and distinct. The left sacred goes from shrine to shrine, adding gods and practices.[80] The right sacred fears

79. I use this term in the older sense (via Nietzsche) as an inherited framework where Christianity propagated Jewish sacred forms, rather than the American Christian belief that Christians are really the "true" inheritors of Judaism.

80. The pre-monotheist peoples in Europe and Africa were both known to constantly mix traditions, to welcome foreign gods, "try them out," and to add them alongside their own. See again Kadmus. (2018). *True To The Earth*. Gods&Radicals Press, especially regarding the constant multiplicity, pluralism, and additive nature of indigenous African and European belief systems.

the dead, death, disease, and all that issues from the body. The left sacred cleans the bodies of the dead (and even lives among them, as the Aghori in India) and cares for the bodies of the diseased, does magic with menstrual blood under the full moon and swallows semen as part of religious rites (the Boborites for example, a Christian gnostic sect.)

The right sacred needs the gods to stay in their "proper" place. The left sacred urges them to spill out into the everyday, through the spontaneous ecstatic and possessory rituals seen in Greek, Roman, and countless African and Asian cultures (see for example the *Neak Ta*, ancestral land spirits displaced by Cambodian textile factories who possessed female workers while on the job).

Most of all, the right sacred needs things kept separate, parcelled out, divided. Its goal is to make sure the everyday is never polluted by the divine world. The right sacred is the secularizing sacred, dividing the world between the transcendent Other (the gods, ancestors, spirits, the dead, and also the animals, plants, and all of material reality, which in animism is also Other) and the mundane, controllable world of humans.

To be clear, the right sacred has a necessary role. As in the words of T.S. Eliot, "mankind cannot bear very much reality." It is the role of the right sacred to appease, to propitiate, to give offerings to the Other in order to ensure the survival of a people. It is the right sacred that creates and then beheads the sacred king who contains within him the will of the gods and the entire divine order.[81]

Without the right sacred, there is only divine forces, and humans are powerless in their midst. But without the left sacred, there is only division, constant propitiation, constant need for apologies for ever increasing offences (as in modern social justice discourse). Without the left sacred there are only walls and fences, everything property, everything in its proper place. The messy and terrifying chaos of the forest is cut back and mown over, the unpredictable rivers once worshiped as gods are straightened and dammed. The needs of humans become the only priority, without thought to what once-divine nature might think about its exploitation. Animals and plants, once seen as sacred Other beings and ancestors, now become mere industrial products wrapped in that ultimate right sacred invention to keep things pure: plastic.

This is ultimately how our understanding of culture and appropriation has gone so wrong, and especially why it increasingly mirrors right-wing and racial separatist views about purity and pollution. The right sacred, having so strongly enforced the boundaries between the mundane and the divine Other, now has only the symbolic representations of what is sacred (or more properly a simulacra of the sacred, a copy whose original has been destroyed or otherwise no longer

81. See again Graeber, D., & Sahlins, M. (2017). *On Kings*. HAU. Also of note, the members of a mystical group created by Georges Bataille and others to explore the left sacred each vowed to be the *Acephale*, the headless one, assuming one of them would agree to cut off another's head. No one would, showing what ultimately happens without the right sacred.

exists) to propitiate. It is thus trapped in the world of empty forms which it itself created, legalistic codes it no longer remembers why it created. The gods and spirits have become mere metaphors, the sacred reduced to "cultural expression." Yet still the right sacred attempts to perform its role, drawing boundaries and policing the borders of symbols, speech, dress, and every other possible transgression.

This is why a white person adopting the cultural forms of others is seen as so offensive to both white nationalists and also to social justice activists. Both groups use only the logic of the right sacred, the fear of the sacred Other polluting or being polluted when it is out of its proper place. The right sacred can only see such transgression as a negative thing, a "sin" for which someone must atone lest some great harm befall society.

But this is also why the commodification of the sacred has occurred and why the deep spiritual hunger that leads to mass markets for "cultural products" exists. The consumer of spiritual products is buying industrially-produced symbols of the sacred, searching for an experience of the transgressive left sacred by the only means available to them—the capitalist market. But in that market, the divine and terrifying Other is reduced to mere profane commodity. This is not the sacred escaping its policed boundaries: in capitalist production, nothing is sacred, everything is profaned.

THE CHAOTIC RETURN OF THE LEFT SACRED

So, how can we reorient these discussions about cultural appropriation towards this understanding of the missing left sacred? Because there is absolutely a justifiable concern from indigenous peoples for the survival of their cultures in the face of domination and extermination.

Before continuing, I'll engage in some personal disclosure. With the exception of Tarot (which is not my primary method of divination, as I use one I created myself) and my passion for cooking "non-European" food, none of my spiritual practices, nor mode of dress or speech, nor any of the gods and spirits I revere and communicate with can be said to be "appropriative." I don't use white sage, I do not wear dreadlocks or bangles or say "lit" or "bae," nor do I use any spiritual forms from any culture other than those of my ancestors. That's not by intended choice nor moral decision: it just happened that way.

Also, though I was born in the United States I no longer live in North America, which in the minds of some means I have no right to speak about the situation there while in the eyes of others I am still a "white American settler" who still somehow benefits from a national situation I specifically chose to flee and intend never to return to.

I disclose all of this to head off several common accusations about anyone arguing for a more nuanced understanding of culture and transgression: "you're just a white person who thinks they can do whatever they want" and "you're just a settler-colonist trying to justify your theft." None of my own practices need defending, and I am not engaged in stealing from or oppressing indigenous people.

My concern, instead, is twofold. First, as I mentioned, the current arguments about cultural appropriation lead to an increasing framework of racial separatism. "White people should not do non-white things," whether said by a white nationalist or a social justice activist, ultimately leads to the same terrifying end, which is ultra-nationalism and fascism.

Secondly, and much more primary, my concern is for the sacred itself. Most arguments about cultural appropriation, especially in the United States, generally skirt around the idea of the sacred. Oftentimes it's quite clear many of the participants on all sides don't actually believe in gods, magic, or spirits, nor do they approach these matters from anything recognizable as an animist framework. That is, the arguments are rarely about what the sacred itself might want or desire or what might give offence to it, but rather what is offensive to other humans or to nebulous people groups.

If one doesn't believe the sacred exists, or if one's conception of the sacred is something relative to an individual or people group rather than something that is in-itself sacred, then the conversations will always be founded instead upon secular political situations and frameworks. If on the other hand a person believes the sacred "really" exists, not just as metaphor or cultural forms, then the conversation will include a line of reasoning that those secular political situations cannot accommodate.

To put it in a much simpler way, consider the sacred oak tree outside my window as I write this. Is the tree sacred because humans made it sacred, or was this tree sacred and I merely recognize its sacred nature? The first view is human-centric and assumes that humans are the arbiters of what is sacred and what is mundane. The second view, which is the animist view, recognizes that there is a divine Other which exists outside, without, and despite us. In this view, the tree is sacred in-itself, not because "all trees are sacred" but because the divine Other intersects through this particular tree's existence and the tree itself is divinely Other.[82]

In the secular, non-animist view, appropriated cultural forms do harm to people and ultimately endanger those forms. In the animist view, the appropriation of cultural forms are a sign of the sacred "transgressing" the boundaries humans made for it, attempting to spread and expand just like forests tend to do. This latter view, the left sacred view, does not necessarily mean that theft should be encouraged. Instead, it concludes that this is part of the nature of the sacred itself, a buried or chthonic shadow aspect.

---

82. Note here that both frameworks at least would agree in one area: the tree should not be cut down because it is sacred.

The divine Other wants always to infect the world, to overwhelm the channels and burst past the dams we build for it. Thus, it is not only not surprising but also quite humorous that gods worshiped in India are inked into the arms of London and Los Angeles hipsters, that sacred entheogenic practices colonial administrators attempted to eradicate are now being practiced in the very nations from which those administrators came. Likewise, it is both unsurprising and also humorous that the gods and ancestors of colonized and oppressed peoples of Africa and the Americas were hidden in plain sight through their syncretic association with Catholic saints (the original meaning of "cultural appropriation"), just as the Pagan gods of European peoples like Brighid, Ana, and Hermes survive in Catholic saints Brigitte, Anne, and Expedite.

Shift the view slightly and we can also find ourselves laughing at the terror of a white Southern Baptist preacher seeing his grandchildren wearing the hairstyles and using the language of the black people he fought to segregate out from "proper" society, just as medieval Catholic bishops complained relentlessly of the faithful dancing the old dances, visiting the old fountains, and even engaging in secret rites with menstrual blood under the full moon.

We must remember here: in the animist view, the sacred cannot be destroyed, because it is wholly-Other. The sacred is a terrible, terrifying, powerful force. Attempts to destroy it, or to suppress it, only make it angry, make it more insistent about transgressing into the mundane.

That, I think, is what is happening now. It is a messy and unclean process, especially politically. The social justice framework cannot accommodate for this sacred resurgence, especially because the sacred cares nothing for modern myths about racial and national identity. There is little we can do about it, as policing the borders of culture only further entrenches the right sacred at the expense of its left.

It has been said that "Rome conquered Greece, but Greece also conquered Rome." The meaning of this phrase is that Rome's occupation and displacement of Greek political power not only did not eradicate Greek culture and belief, but instead caused it to be transformed, "polluted" in the left sacred sense, by Greek gods, Greek magical systems, Greek philosophy, and thus ultimately by Greek-ness itself. Roman temples were copies of Greek temples, most Roman religious forms and even gods were transparent copies of the Greek forms and gods they "conquered."

Perhaps we are seeing this again. Empire (capitalist, secular/Christian, "western" and especially American Empire) conquered the world and is still fighting constantly to eradicate the sacred from the earth. But the sacred cannot be eradicated, only enclosed for a little while and temporarily appeased. The colonialist order is being colonized by those Empire tried to subjugate, along with their beliefs, their gods, their cultural and ancestral traditions. And most of all, the Sacred itself is poised to destroy all our fragile notions of purity and separation, of what is proper and what is property, until the left sacred finally can take its true place alongside the right.

RHYD WILDERMUTH

Rhyd is a druid, a writer, and a theorist. He was born in the foothills of the Appalachian mountains but now lives in a forested valley of the Ardennes.

Being Pagan is his sixth book. He is also the author of *The Provisioner, All That is Sacred Is Profaned, Witches in a Crumbling Empire, A Kindness of Ravens,* and *Your Face Is a Forest*, all from Gods&Radicals Press and RITONA Press.

He also writes frequently at *From The Forests of Arduinna* (rhyd.substack.com), and whiles much of his time with words, with plants, with his bike, with weightlifting, and with his partner.